To: Mr. & Mr...
From: I. & I. ...
Christmas, 1966.
Le Beannachd.

The Spouting Cave

IONA : A HISTORY OF THE ISLAND

With Descriptive Notes

By

F. MARIAN McNEILL, M.A.

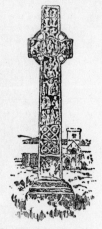

St. Martin's Cross, Iona.

BLACKIE & SON LIMITED
LONDON AND GLASGOW

BLACKIE & SON LIMITED
5 Fitzhardinge Street
London, W.1
17 Stanhope Street, Glasgow

BLACKIE & SON (INDIA) LIMITED
103/5 Fort Street, Bombay

By the Same Author:

The Scots Kitchen: Its Traditions and
Lore, with Old-time Recipes.

First issued 1920
Reprinted 1923, 1930, 1934
Second edition 1935
Reprinted 1937, 1939
Third edition 1946
Reprinted 1947, 1949, 1951
Fourth edition 1954
Reprinted 1955
Fifth edition 1959

Printed in Great Britain by Blackie & Son, Ltd., Glasgow

PREFACE TO FIFTH EDITION

When I visited Iona in 1917 I tried to obtain a modest handbook which should give a concise and comprehensive account of the island: its history and significance in the progress of our Western civilization; its antiquities of the Celtic and mediæval periods; and, not least, its folk-lore, which gives life and colour to almost every nook and cranny in the little island. But although all this ground had been covered admirably, and with much detail—notably in Trenholme's *Story of Iona*, to which, and to Macmillan and Brydall's *Iona: Its History and Antiquities*, I am indebted for much information regarding the antiquities and topography of the island—a small handbook at a popular price was lacking. I have tried here to compile the book I vainly sought, and trust it will meet the need which many others have felt.

Since this book was first issued, an outstanding event in the modern history of Iona has taken place—the institution on the island of the Iona Community. Its aims and methods are briefly described on p. 53.

In recent years, researches into the antiquities of Iona and the history of the early Celtic Church have proceeded, various buildings on the island have been restored, and other improvements made. In this new edition, I have made such emendations and additions as were required to bring my book up to date.

I desire to express my indebtedness to the late Alexander and Mrs. Ritchie of Iona and to Dr. D. J. Macleod of Inverness for the help they have given me.

The photographs included are by Mr. Donald B. MacCulloch and Mr. Tom Weir, to whom I am grateful for allowing me to use them.

F. MARIAN McNEILL.

Edinburgh, 1959.

To

HELEN WEIR MICKEL

who first directed my steps to Iona

CONTENTS

LIST OF ILLUSTRATIONS

Sketch Map of Scotland at the Time of Columba

IONA

I

Introductory

In the midst of the Hebrides or Western Isles of Scotland lies a little island, fashioned of rock and heather, on which the Atlantic seas beat ceaselessly. So small and modest is its aspect, so undistinguishable amongst its myriad sister isles, that the traveller who has not fully learned the secret of its spell may well marvel at its power to draw and hold the homage of men of many lands and creeds and centuries.

Thirteen hundred years ago, on the last day of his life, St. Columba, whose name is forever bound with that of Iona, ascended the little hill overlooking the monastery, and blessed the island, saying:

" Unto this place, small and mean though it be, great homage shall yet be paid, not only by the kings and peoples of the Scots, but by the rulers of barbarous and distant nations with their people. Thy saints also, of other churches, shall regard it with no common reverence."

This prophecy has been remarkably fulfilled. And not only did the centuries provide a continuous stream of travellers from over the civilized world, but for many generations the bodies of princes and chiefs were brought hither to lie in its hallowed soil. The procession of the dead has long since ceased, but still the pilgrims come.

To the traveller, who would not let the glamour and significance of Iona escape him, as they escape many, it is well to emphasize that he will find no stimulus to his imagination in wild, awe-inspiring scenery or imposing array of ancient ruins. Natural beauty the island assuredly possesses, but it is a beauty so demure, so winsome, that it is apt to evade those whose taste inclines to a more exotic type. But for those who have eyes to see, there is a subtle beauty in the apparent barrenness: a beauty mainly of atmosphere: a beauty part physical, part spiritual. The ruins themselves, though lacking grandeur of dimension and luxuriance of setting, yet show to the initiated such beauty of design and skill in workmanship as justify their wide renown.

The attitude of mind of the voyager to Iona is all-important, and for that he must know something of its place in the spiritual history of the world. " Let us approach that sacred isle ", writes Bishop Ewing, " with more than common reverence: there where it now lies in the midst of rolling billows, and listening but to sea-birds' cries, from age to age in the morning of early history, night and day it heard the sweet songs of God."

" Since the remotest days," writes Fiona Macleod, " sacrosanct men have bowed here in worship. In this little isle a lamp was lit whose flame lighted pagan Europe. . . . Here Learning and Faith had their tranquil home, when the shadow of the sword lay upon all lands. . . . From age to age lowly hearts have never ceased to bring their burden there."

Even Dr. Johnson, that sturdy Saxon and unlikely pilgrim to such a spot, was moved to write one of his finest (if now most hackneyed) apostrophes on Iona:

" We are now treading that illustrious isle which was once the luminary of the Caledonian regions, whence savage clans and roving barbarians derived the benefits of knowledge and the blessings of religion. To abstract the mind from all local emotion would be impossible if it were endeavoured, and would be foolish if it were possible. Whatever withdraws us from the power of our senses, whatever makes the past, the distant, or the future predominate over the present, advances us in the dignity of thinking beings. Far from me and my friends be such frigid philosophy as may conduct us, indifferent and unmoved, over any ground which has been dignified by wisdom, bravery or virtue. That man is little to be envied whose patriotism would not gain force upon the plains of Marathon, or whose piety would not grow warmer among the ruins of Iona."

Iona is a very small island—about three miles long and one or more in breadth—situated off the west coast of Argyllshire, and separated from the south-west coast of Mull by a narrow sound about half a mile across. It has a lovely setting in the blue Hebridean seas, which stretch, island-studded, to a far horizon. Immediately to the north are the rocky Treshnish Islands, and Staffa, with its great cathedral caves. Farther off lie the long, low island of Tiree, which was cultivated by Columba's monks when Iona itself was no longer able to support the growing community; the mountain-island of Rum, where a hermit-monk once made his cell; the beautiful isle of Eigg, where St. Donnan, the one martyr of the early Celtic Church, met his doom at the instigation of a Pictish queen; the jagged outline of the Coolins in Skye; and a dim speck that is Barra. Due east of Iona is the large island of Mull, with its misty mountains, its shadowy lochs, and its great deserted glens, once brimming with human life, but now the home of the red deer. To the south-east, beyond the red granite cliffs of the Ross of Mull, is the rounded outline of the Paps of Jura, with Colonsay in the fore-ground and Islay just beyond. Southward, some seventy miles distant and beyond the range of the eye, is the coast of Ireland. West of Iona, the vast Atlantic stretches for two thousand miles in an unbroken sweep to the shores of Labrador.

The island itself is low-lying, with numerous, irregular elevations which rarely exceed a hun-dred feet, though Dùn-I (pronounced Doon-ee) approaches four hundred. For its size Iona contains much variety of feature. A belt of arable land crosses the middle of the island, and a tract of it lies to the north of the Cathedral. Elsewhere, among the crags and heather, the great-horned, shaggy Highland cattle find ex-cellent pasturage. To the south lie stretches of boggy moorland, and on the heights are rocks " that wade in heather, and upon whose brows the sea-wind waves the yellow lichen ".— (Fiona Macleod). The coast-line is similarly varied: there are cliff and cave and sheltered bay, and to the north lies a great stretch of dazzling silver sand.

The landscape is treeless, though a few small

trees have been reared in gardens; but there
is a wonderful variety of wild flowers. The
little yellow St. John's Wort (Hypericum) is
reputed to have been St. Columba's favourite
flower, owing perhaps to its shape, which suggests a cross. There are various land-birds,
but cliff- and sea-birds predominate. These
include the beautiful oyster-catcher, named
in Gaelic *gille-brigde*, the servant of Bride.
Seals, those soft-eyed creatures which, according to Gaelic tradition, are human beings under
a spell, come sometimes to meditate on the
lonelier beaches. There are no vipers on the
island, though they are plentiful just across
the sound in Mull. Tradition credits Columba
with the immunity of the island in this respect,
but a more modern explanation is the quality
of the soil.

The population of the island is roughly two
hundred. Agriculture is the main occupation
of the islanders, though they take their toll
also of the sea, which abounds in flounders
and saith. The sea-tangle supplies the island
with manure, and the dulse has culinary uses.
In the winter months the spinning-wheel hums
by the fireside, the whole process from the
shearing of the sheep—the dyeing with roots
and sea-weeds, the carding, the spinning—to
the weaving on hand-looms, being carried out
by the island craftsfolk.

The climate in winter is mild, and snow is rare, but the island is subject to fierce gales which sometimes cut off all communication for days at a stretch. Even in summer, one cannot always escape that bane of the West Highlands, a prolonged rainfall. Yet it is said that when the islands are tempest-ridden, and the mountains of Mull are cloaked in gloom, on Iona itself there is always a brightness.

On a clear summer day, and particularly when the wind is in the north the beauty is idyllic. Soft cirrous clouds veil the blue vault of heaven. Over the wide, white sands the sea glistens green as an emerald; farther out it is of vivid blue, barred with purple. The granite cliffs of Mull glow rosy across the Sound, and the great mountains beyond cast their deep-blue shadow on the still waters. There is a wealth of colour, not gorgeous, but exquisite, appealing less to the senses than to the spirit, and creating a sense of peace that is balm to the world-weary. The pilgrim, the antiquarian, the artist: Iona casts her spell on all.

A note on the geology of Iona, which is remarkable. The island is immeasurably older, not only than the surrounding islands, but also than the highest mountains and most of the dry land on the earth. During the great earth-changes of the Tertiary period, the face of the globe attained, with minor differences, its present configuration. But "the beginning of Iona is almost part of the beginning of the world itself. When our planet, from a flaming mass of combustion like the sun, shrivelled into a globe with a solid crust, and the first oceans condensed in the hollows of its surface—then it was that the Archæan rocks of which Iona and the Outer Hebrides consist were formed on the sea bottom. They contain no fossils; for, so far as is known, no living creature as yet existed in the desolate waste of waters, or on the primeval land. They were hard, rugged, and twisted; and in Iona, as elsewhere, marble has been developed by the vast heat and pressure they have undergone. . . . The great Ice Age has also left its mark, for the glaciers from the hills of Mull reached out over the Sound, and, as they melted, boulders of red granite, scraped from the Ross, dropped out of the ice along the eastern shore of Iona, where they still lie, both large and small."—(Trenholme: *Story of Iona*.)

Iona was originally called Ioua, its ancient Gaelic or Pictish name. This is the name invariably used by Adamnan, the ninth Abbot, writing at the end of the seventh century. Other old spellings are: Eo, Ea, Io, Ia. In modern Gaelic it is called I (pronounced *ee*), the island, and also Y, Hy, Hi, and Hii. Owing to its close association with Columba, the saint's name was often linked on to that of the island, making, in anglicized Gaelic, Icolmkill, the island of Colum of the Church. Another name is *Innis nam Druineach*, meaning the Island of the Cunning Workmen, or sculptors; and still another is *Innis-nam-Druidneach*, the Isle of Druids. The story that Iona was a sacred isle of Druids before Columba's time seems to have sprung up at a late period, but the word *druid* is still used occasionally in speaking of ministers and priests, and the name may mean " the isle of priests ".

There is a theory that " Iona " is derived from *I-shona*, which, as the initial letters *sh* are invariably mute in Gaelic, is pronounced Iona, and which means " the isle of saints ".

The generally accepted view, however, is that the name Iona is derived from the original Ioua, through the mistake of mediæval scribes in the copying of manuscripts, and that the word got thus into English and Latin, though not into Gaelic use.

It is worthy of note that the Hebrew word *Iona* corresponds to the Latin *Columba*, meaning " a dove ".

II

Scotland before Columba

In pre-Christian days, the religion of the
Celtic race, of whose ancient territory Ireland
and Scotland formed part, was Druidism.
The origins of this religion are lost in antiquity, and indeed we have little authentic
knowledge at all concerning it; for it was
esoteric, hidden, and its unwritten doctrine
and ritual disappeared with the last of the
ancient priesthood. St. Patrick, St. Columba,
and other Celtic saints have little or nothing
to say of the faith which it was their mission
to supersede.

The pre-Christian Celts, like other ancient
races, sought " the unknown God " in their
own manner. They worshipped the rising
sun, kept the feast of Beltane, on May Day,
with sun-worship and fire-ceremonies, celebrated All-Hallow-E'en, and reverenced the
mistletoe. There is no evidence that the
Pictish Druids offered human sacrifices and
taught transmigration of souls, as did the
Druids of Gaul.

(D 58)

The Communion Table

Interior,
Abbey Church

The old religion appears to have had three orders, for which men were trained in the Colleges of Initiates. These included the Druid proper, whose temple was a spreading oak and whose altar a stone; the Bard, whose office was to preserve and hand on the national tradition; and the Seer, who foretold the future by the position of the stars and the flight of birds. There was probably much that was beautiful in the old religion, but in its later period it appears to have become degraded into a religion of witchcraft. " It was a vague dread of innumerable spirits; the world of nature was quivering with life; in every spring and well there was a spirit; in every loch there lived some dreaded being. When the echoes of thunder rolled through the mountain corries, or when the wild storm beat the forests of oak, voices from the great Mystery were speaking." The Druids of Columba's time were an official class of diviners and sorcerers who professed to have powers over this spirit world, and to be able to direct the wind and weather and avert the enmity of evil spirits by means of charms and spells.

(There have been some curious survivals of pagan worship. In Iona, for example, down to the end of the eighteenth century, a solemn ceremony took place on the midnight preceding Maunday Thursday, when the " great porridge " was cast into the western bay as an offering to the sea, that it might wash up enough seaweed for the second spring ploughing.)

Yet, in spite of the darkness that prevailed at the time of Columba's coming, the task of the Christian missionaries in Druidical countries was far less arduous than in those lands where personal or representative gods were worshipped; for the nature-worship of the Druids was not so incompatible with Christianity as the definite polytheistic systems of antiquity. The contest between the Druids and the emissaries of Christianity was keen, but it was singularly free from fanaticism and violence, and we have no record of martyrdoms such as characterize the later history of the Christian Church.

Columba found in the land of his adoption " a people with a love of the arts and a passion for music, a people steeped in that mysticism, that dominating sense of the unseen without which religion is mere ignorant superstition, with that conviction of the close environment of the spiritual world that still characterizes their descendents to a greater or less degree. . . . It needed but the trump of Christianity and the colleges became monasteries, the wells and sacred haunts were dedicated to the saints, . . . the revered oak tree associated with Our Lady."—(Wilkie.)

Although Iona became the " lamp of Christ whose flame lighted pagan Europe ", other lights, though mostly dim and obscure, had previously glimmered on these islands. How Christianity was first brought to our shores is not clearly known, but it appears to have come direct from the East. In these far-off days the Celtic Church, like the Roman Church, was regarded as one of the many secondary sources of Christianity, of which Jerusalem was recognized as the fountainhead. Rome was pagan for three centuries after Christ, and in that period these early forerunners of Columba and Augustine had already penetrated to our islands. We know little or nothing about them, save that their work was practically undone by the invading hordes of the pagan Jutes, Angles, and Saxons in the fifth and sixth centuries.

Palladius is said to have been the earliest missionary to Scotland. He was closely followed by St. Ninian (born *circa* 350) who laboured among the southern Picts in Galloway. After Ninian came St. Patrick (born, as most scholars now agree, at Dunbriton or Dumbarton), who brought Christianity to Ireland, and established there a great school of piety and learning which was destined to produce Columba. Other saints were meanwhile at work in Scotland, but their influence was

local and temporary.   Even Ninian's converts
became demoralized, and the country as a whole
remained wrapt in pagan gloom.[1]

Of one of these early missionaries, St. Mochta,
it is related that he laboured long and fruit-
lessly in North Britain, and returned at last
to Ireland.   Here his labours were crowned
with success, which, however, did not obliterate
the memory of his earlier defeat.   It was ob-
served that the saint, discarding the custom
of his time to pray toward the east, prayed
always towards the north, and he was asked
the reason.   He replied that at the end of a
hundred years out of the north would come
a dove.

The coming of Columba was predicted also
by St. Patrick and St. Bride.

When Columba was born, though the bar-
barian tribes had descended on Rome, the
Empire still stood.   Justinian was emperor;
Benedict had established his order at Monte

---

[1] Recent researches reveal that Ninian accomplished much
more than has hitherto been accredited to him, his foundations
having been traced all over the south and east of Scotland and as
far north as Caithness. Broadly speaking, Ninian may be regarded
as the apostle of the Picts and Columba as the apostle of the Scots,
their main spheres of labour lying respectively east and west of
Drumalbain (the ridge that traverses the Scottish Highlands from
north to south). Ninian, in short, can no longer be dismissed as
a mere forerunner of Columba, but shares with him the glory of
Christianizing Scotland, Columba's great achievement being to
complement and consolidate the work of the earlier saint.

Cassino; Gregory was a law student at Rome; Mahomet was not yet born. Europe was in a state of violent upheaval, and the great nations of to-day had not yet emerged. The Saxon tribes were invading and paganizing the land that is now England, and driving the British tribes westward to the mountains. Ireland, standing apart, escaped the general devastation and became the asylum of learning.

What is now Scotland was divided into several small principalities: North and south of the Grampians were the Northern and Southern Picts; in the south-west were the Britons of Strathclyde and the Picts of Galloway; in the south-east were a group of English settlers (Angles), probably the only non-Celtic race in Scotland, whose king fortified the rock of Edwin's Burg or Edinburgh; and, lastly, there was a colony of Scots, or Gaelic Celts, who had crossed from Ireland in the fifth century and spread over what is now Argyll (land of the Gael) and the adjacent isles. These Scots, to which race Columba belonged, were Christian, and were destined to give to the land of their adoption its name, its royal house, and its religion.

At this period the Celtic name of Scotland was Alban, and the Latin name Scotia was applied only to Ireland, called also Hibernia.

III

Columba in Ireland

Of the lives of Ninian, Bride, and Patrick, and
even of Columba's contemporary, St. Mungo,
we have scanty knowledge, but of Columba's
achievements a remarkably clear record exists.
Adamnan's *Life of St. Columba* is one of the
treasures of history, and " the most complete
piece of such biography that Europe can boast
of, not only at so early a period, but even through
the whole Middle Ages ".—(Pinkerton: *Lives
of Scottish Saints*.) It was written in Iona
by Adamnan, the ninth Abbot, at the urgent
request, as he tells us, of the brethren. The
biographer was born in 624, twenty-seven years
after the death of the saint. He conversed
with men who had been Columba's monks,
had access to all the literary remains, and em-
bodied in his book the fragmentary record
of an earlier Abbot. The book is in part
hagiology rather than biography, and the reader
must make what allowances his training and
temperament demand for the prophetic and
miraculous elements in the narrative.

Columba was born on 4th December, 521, at Gartan, a wild, mountainous district in Donegal, the haunt of the wolf, and, to this day, of the eagle. He was descended from the royal house of Neill, his father, Phelim MacFergus, being a great-grandson of Niall of the Nine Hostings, High King of Ireland at Royal Tara from 379 to 405. In Niall's day, Ireland was a pagan land, but a certain British lad, named Patrick, was a slave in Connaught. Patrick escaped to Gaul, and in the course of time returned to Ireland, which he converted from Druidism to Christianity, and of which he became later the patron saint. Niall's son, Conall, Columba's great-grandfather, was baptized by St. Patrick.

Columba's mother, Eithne, was also of royal descent. The old Irish life of the saint says that he was eligible for the throne of Erin, which would have been offered him had he not abandoned it for the service of Christ.

There is a legend that, before her son was born, Eithne dreamed one night that an angel stood before her and offered her a robe of exquisite beauty. Scarcely was it hers than the angel took it from her and spread it out till it covered mountain and lough and forest, reaching even to Scotland. From this sign Eithne knew that her child was the child of the prophecies, and destined to lead innumerable souls to Heaven.

Columba's education was accordingly directed to fit him for his mission. He received two names: Crimthan, a wolf, and Colum, a dove, each of which seems appropriate to one element of his complex character. His early education was entrusted to Cruithnechan, an aged presbyter, renowned for sanctity, who lived near by. The child's love for the offices of the church was so marked that the children of the neighbourhood, whom he would join on coming from the cell in which he read his psalms, named him Columcille, Colum of the cell or church. Columba is, of course, the Latin form of Colum.

When his fosterage under Cruithnechan was ended, Columba was placed under the care of Finnian at an ecclesiastical school in Moville, where he was ordained deacon. Thence he proceeded to Leinster, where he studied the native literature under Gemman, the venerable Bard of that province. According to Irish tradition, he retained throughout his life the love he there acquired for the old, poetic tales of his race; and, himself a poet, he probably became a member of the Order of Bards. From Master Gemman, he went on to the monastic school of St. Finnian—the most famous school in Ireland—situated by the waters of the Boyne.

Finally, after a period at the monastery of Glasnevin, near Dublin, where he probably pronounced his monastic vow, he returned to his native Ulster.

In 545, Columba founded the monastery of Derry on a site given him by his kinsmen of the Clan Neill. He came to realize, however, that monasticism did not fully satisfy the needs of the time. Refreshed with a period of prayer and fasting—a visit, too, to Tours, in Gaul, took place about this time—he left Derry, and began to preach up and down Ireland, attacking paganism where it still existed, and strengthening the faith in other parts. Everywhere he founded churches, of which over three hundred are ascribed to him; and monasteries, of which the most famous are Durrow and Kells. The power of organization was one of his many gifts, and Scotland reaped the fruits of his Irish experience. His method was to find a suitable site where a church was needed, and go boldly to the owner and ask for it; then, when permission was given, he erected the requisite buildings—not scrupling to work with his own hands when necessary—installed carefully trained workers and passed on; and, in spite of his constant journeyings, he continued to keep in touch with all his foundations.

Why Columba left Ireland for Scotland is not known with certainty. A popular account

has it that the saint, who was a fervent scribe
and highly skilled in the art of illumination,
secretly copied for his own use a beautiful
manuscript of the book of Psalms, belonging
to his old master, Finnian of Moville. The
owner demanded the copy, which was refused.
Finnian appealed to Diarmaid, King of Ireland,
and chief of the southern Clan Neill. The
king gave judgment in these words: " To
every cow belongs her calf, and to every book
its copy ". Columba, filled with wrath at the
decision, incited his kinsmen of the northern
Clan Neill to battle, and Diarmaid was defeated
with great slaughter. Columba was then
summoned by Diarmaid before a synod and
excommunicated; but the sentence was afterwards annulled. Full of remorse for his deed,
Columba sought his " anmcara ", his soul-
friend or spiritual adviser, who counselled him
that, as a penance, he should go into perpetual
exile, and win as many souls for Christ as he
had caused bodies to be slain in battle.

This narrative is not reliable. Adamnan not
only does not mention it, but he speaks of
Columba's having revisited Ireland on ten
different occasions. It is more likely that his
departure from Ireland was concerned with
the position of his kinsfolk in the Scottish
Dalriada (Argyllshire), so named after the
Irish Dalriada (Antrim), whence they came.

(The channel which separates the two countries is only twelve miles wide, and the houses in Kintyre can be seen from the Irish coast opposite). The northern Picts were at this time a barbarous and pagan race; the southern Britons had lapsed sadly since the days of Ninian; and the Scots were the only Christian people in North Britain. In 560 the Scots settlers suffered a crushing defeat at the hands of Brude, King of the Northern Picts; their king, a kinsman of Columba, was slain; and there was a danger that the whole colony might be extirpated. In Skene's opinion (and in accordance with a prophecy in the Chronicle of the Picts and Scots) it was this reverse which called forth the mission of St. Columba, and led him to select North Pictland as his first field. Christianity was to be the bond which should unite these turbulent nations, and establish among them an abiding peace.

Adamnan puts the reason for Columba's departure quite simply: " In the forty-second year of his age, desiring to seek a foreign country for the sake of Christ, he sailed from Ireland to Britain ".

IV

Iona

In 563, Columba, accompanied by twelve followers, sailed from Derry in a frail coracle of wicker and hides. After visiting his kinsmen in the Scottish Dalriada, he continued his journey northwards. According to tradition, he landed first on Oronsay, but, on discovering that his fatherland was still in sight, he re-embarked, and set his prow for Iona. On the hill a little westward of Port à Churaich, the Bay of the Coracle, where Columba landed, is a small cairn, called Carn Cul ri Eirinn, the Cairn of-the-back-to-Erin. Here, it is said, Columba scanned the southern horizon, and, satisfied that his beloved land was out of sight, buried the coracle on the beach, and entered into possession.

Iona was, in most respects, admirably suited for Columba's purpose. Its position on the line which divided the Christian Scots of Argyll from the pagan Picts made it a convenient strategic centre for mission work. It had also natural advantages, as the late Duke of Argyll

points out in his little book, *Iona*. "On the
eastern side was the channel which he had
missed, giving much-needed shelter from prevailing winds. Above all, it was a fertile island,
giving promise of ample sustenance for man
and beast. It is true Iona is a rocky island,
the bones protruding at frequent intervals
through the skin of turf. Even there, however, Columba must have seen that the pasture
was close and good, and not far from the spot
on which he first swept the southern sky he
must have found that the heathy and rocky
hills subsided into a lower tract, green with
that delicious turf which, full of thyme and
wild clover, gathers upon soils of shelly sand.
This tract is called in Gaelic the ' Machair ' or
Sandy Plain. A little farther on he must soon
have found that the eastern or sheltered side
presented a slope of fertile soil exactly suiting
the essential conditions of ancient husbandry
—a tract of land which was as admirably
adapted for the growth of corn as the re-
mainder of it was suited to the support of
flocks and herds."

According to the Irish annals, the island was
granted to Columba by Conall, the sixth king
of the Scottish Dalriada; according to the
venerable Bede, it was granted by Brude, King
of the Northern Picts. "The probability is ",
says Huyshe, " that Columba found Iona un-

occupied and unclaimed, that Conall promised not to disturb his occupation of it, and that, when the Picts were converted to Christianity by Columba, King Brude sanctioned his right and title to the little island."

Loyal workers from Ireland speedily followed the pioneers, and soon the island was as busy as a hive.

Of the buildings erected by Columba not a trace remains save one or two individual stones, such as the Saint's Pillow, which will be mentioned later. The ruins of to-day date only from the Middle Ages, and even the traces of a still earlier monastery are of much later date than Columba. The original buildings were constructed on the Irish model, and were probably a mere collection of huts composed of timber and wattle, surrounded by a vallum of earth. We can picture it fairly clearly from Adamnan's references: the oaken church with the sacristy adjoining it; the refectory with its fire-place and its stone vessel of water where the feet of tired pilgrims were washed, the kitchen near by; the guest chamber; the mill, the barn, the stable; the individual huts of the monks arranged round the enclosures; and, a little apart, the hut of the Abbot.

" The glory of these buildings was within," says Riley. " It is by no means impossible ", he goes on, " that the severe simplicity, as well as the uniformity of plan and size, which usually characterize our early churches, was less the result of the poverty or ignorance of their founders than of choice, originating in the spirit of their faith, or veneration for some model given them by their first teachers; for that the earliest Christian churches on the continent before the time of Constantine were like these, small and unadorned, there is no reason to doubt."

The rule of the monastery in Iona, as in Ireland, enforced strict observance of religious duty, and ascetic practice. Obedience, Celibacy, Poverty, Caution and Reason in Speech, and Humility, these were its main features; and specially characteristic of Iona, Hospitality and Kindness to Animals. The monks called their Abbot Father; to him they were children, to one another brethren, and from the earliest times the community is spoken of as the Family of Hy.

The first two years of Columba's residence in Iona were spent in learning the language, tilling the soil, training followers, and generally in organizing the community. The days were filled with prayer, study, and manual labour, and in this last Columba, with his great spiritual and intellectual gifts, was always ready to share. " In dairy, granary, or in the fields, each worshipped God in his appointed task,

and made his toil a sacramental thing."—
(Troup.)

But these men were not recluses, and monastic routine did not satisfy them. The Columban Church was a missionary church, and
its founder was preparing his followers for
the great enterprise of converting an entirely
pagan land to Christianity. His plan was to
begin by attacking Pictish paganism in its
stronghold, at the court of Brude at Inverness,
and when the time was ripe he set forth with
two carefully chosen comrades, St. Kenneth
and St. Comgall, both Irish Picts, who knew
the language of Brude's court.

The route lay due north-east, through the
Great Glen of Alban, with its continuous line
of long, narrow lochs, now linked by the Caledonian Canal. So wild a region, with its dark,
brooding mountains and primeval forests, could
be traversed only on foot, and the whole adventure must have involved the " perils of
water, perils of robbers, perils by the heathen,
perils in the wilderness ", known to the Apostles
of old. They reached their destination without hurt, but Brude, encouraged by Broichan,
the chief Druid, refused them admittance.
At the sign of the Cross, however—so the
legend has it—the bolted gates flew open, and
the awestruck king capitulated. Be that as
it may, it is certain that Brude was won by

the message of Columba, and embraced the Christian religion. Thus did the powerful King of Picts, the race which had withstood the legions of Rome herself, succumb to three soldiers of Christ.

To have converted the Pictish king was nominally to have converted the Pictish people, but Columba's aim was to establish a living faith throughout the land. Bands of trained workers came on from Iona, and there ensued years of untiring labour during which Brude remained a staunch friend. By precept and example the Picts were gradually won over; churches were built; and in every valley Columba placed some " sentry for Christ ".

The political effects of Columba's mission are not to be ignored. His royal descent and his kinship with the noblest families of Ireland and the Scottish Dalriada would alone have made him a power politically; but, apart from this, the first ten years of his labours in Scotland established him as a statesman no less than as a religious leader of uncommon gifts. In winning the Picts to Christianity he had secured peace between the tribes, and prepared the way for political union. His reputation for wisdom and saintliness was now such that he was frequently called upon to settle disputes between the clans; the King of Strathclyde sent to consult him regarding his future;

and when the King of the Scottish Dalriada
died, it was Columba who appointed his successor, Aidan, who went to Iona for consecra-
tion at the saint's hands. (This is the earliest
record of a royal coronation in Great Britain.)
In 575, at the famous Convention of Drumceatt
in Ireland, Columba accomplished three objects
of note: first, the " staying " of the Bards, whose
sentence of expulsion because of their annoying
exactions of hospitality, he had replaced by the
imposition of restrictive rules, thus preserving
a great Irish institution; secondly, the exemption
of women from military service; and, thirdly,
the political independence of the Scottish Dalriada, thus settling a long-standing quarrel
between the Irish king and the King of Argyll.

Columba has been accredited with martial
propensities, and according to tradition was concerned in more than one battle fought on Irish
soil. Dr. Reeves, commenting on this, says
that we must bear in mind the complexion of the
times and the peculiar condition of society,
of which civil faction seemed almost part and
parcel.

When the Northern and Southern Picts were
united, Columba sent his missionaries south-
wards as far as the Forth and the Clyde. South
of this another saint was at work: Kentigern
—better known as Mungo, the Beloved One
—far-famed for the austere simplicity of his

life. The saint had been trained at the school of St. Serf in Fife, and had made his centre at Cathures, now Glasgow. In one of his missionary journeys Columba was able to satisfy a long-felt desire to visit his unknown brother. " When Mungo heard that the Apostle of the North was near at hand, he marshalled his little company; the children led the way, followed by the novices, then the older monks, and then the holy man himself. . . . As the two processions drew near, one company chanted the portion of a psalm, and from the others in the distance came the response."— (Troup.) After enjoying Mungo's frugal hospitality for many days, Columba departed, the saints having exchanged pastoral staves in token of their mutual love of Christ.

The places visited and churches founded in Columba's lifetime all over the mainland and the isles are too numerous to count. Daughter monasteries arose, but Iona remained the " citadel and retreat " of the Celtic missionaries.

The monks must have been skilled and daring navigators. Adamnan mentions several types of boats belonging to the island fleet: the coracle of wicker and hide, the bark, the skiff, the cobble, the freight-ship, and the long boat hollowed out of a single oak or pine tree. The most famous of the sailor-monks was

Cormac, who penetrated to Orkney and Shetland, and, it is thought probable, to the Faröes and Iceland. Columba himself, like all Celts, loved the sea, and long after his death was invoked by sailors in storm. " He who is wise with the wisdom of a hundred storms ", says Kenneth Macleod, " will have two tillers to his rudder: the Art of the Druids for the luck of Wind, and the Faith of Iona for the stilling of the Waves."

It is not known how long before his death Columba ceased travelling. From work he never ceased, and in later years he probably gave much of his time to the copying of manuscripts, an art in which he was highly skilled. Two splendid manuscripts are commonly attributed to him — the *Cathach*, a Psalter (in the Library of the Royal Irish Academy), and the *Book of Durrow*, the Gospels (in the Library of Trinity College, Dublin). He was not only a scribe but a poet, and probably a member of the Order of Bards which he defended at Drumceatt. Of the large poetical output attributed to him, three fine Latin hymns and several poems in his native Gaelic are preserved.

Stories of Columba's visionary powers abound in Adamnan's pages. In our modern civilization, what is called " second sight " is generally regarded as mere superstition:

yet even amongst the classes we call educated, and especially in our " Celtic fringes ",
there are not a few who believe it to be " a
quickened inward vision ", a veritable sixth
sense, as real as the physical senses, or more
so. " The faculty itself is so apt to the spiritual
law," says Fiona Macleod, " that one wonders
why it is so set apart in doubt." To one who
marvelled at his power, Columba made reply:
" Heaven has granted to some to see on occasion
in their mind, clearly and surely, the whole
of earth and sea and sky."

Adamnan records of Columba that " he
could not pass the space even of a single hour
without applying himself either to prayer, or
reading, or writing, or else to some manual
labour ". He tells us how children loved him
—one climbed to his knee in a poor man's
house—and how the saint loved animals—
he sent a monk to tend a storm-tossed crane
alighted from Ireland, till after three days it
was ready to fly forth. When Columba was
more or less tied by frailty to the island—save
for his retreats to Hinba (Elachnave), an islet
where a monastery for recluses and penitents
existed, and where Eithne, the saint's mother,
is said to be interred — many came from far
distances to seek help and counsel. Pilgrims
of all degrees were constantly ferried across
the strait from Mull by the monks of Iona.

To the end Columba was lord and servant of all.

In the month of May, in the seventy-seventh year of his life, Columba, too feeble to walk the distance between the monastery and the field where the monks were at work, was carried over to the Machar in a cart, and here he told the sorrowing brethren that his end was at hand. On a Saturday in early June, he set forth with his faithful servant Diormit, and took leave of the old familiar places. In the granary he blessed the store of grain, and as he returned to the monastery he rested half-way, at a spot where a cross was afterwards placed. Here, Adamnan tells us, the old white horse that used to carry the milk-pails between the byre and the monastery came up and put its head in the Abbot's lap, whinnying, and shedding copious tears; and when Diormit tried to drive him away, Columba stayed his attendant's hand, and " blessed his sorrowing servant the horse ".

He then ascended the little hill overlooking the monastery, and blessed the island, uttering the prophetic words quoted on the first page of this book. Returning to his cell, he sat transcribing the Psalter, but when he got as far as verse 10 of Psalm xxxiv: " They that seek the Lord shall not want any good thing ", he stopped, saying: " Let Baithen finish it ".

Resting on his bed after vespers that evening, he gave Diormit a message to the brethren: " This, dear children, is my last message to you—that you preserve with each other sincere charity and peace."

When the midnight bell tolled for nocturns, he rose with a last effort, and made his way to the church. Diormit, full of dread, followed his master, calling: " Where art thou, Father?" Groping his way in the darkness, he found the saint lying before the altar, and laid the holy head on his lap. The monks came running with lights, and at the sight of their dying master fell a-weeping. His face lit with joy, the saint made a feeble movement of benediction, " and immediately breathed forth his spirit ".

After three days of vigil, his remains were interred in a simple grave, in the manner of the time.

V

The Celtic Church

The Lamp that Lighted Pagan Europe

The Celtic Church established by Columba in Scotland in the sixth century endured until the death of Malcolm Canmore in the eleventh, when it gave place to the Church of Rome; and even after the religious revolution of that period, the Culdees, a body of Celtic ecclesiastics, can be traced down to the fourteenth century.

The Venerable Bede, a contemporary and friend of Adamnan, tells us that Columba " left successors distinguished for their great charity, divine love, and strict attention to discipline ". For many generations, indeed, that marching soul led men to great enterprises and successful issues. From Scotland, the Iona missionaries passed to England and the continent of Europe. They it was, along with their brothers from Ireland, who brought Christianity to the greater part of Germany and Switzerland, and even to part of Italy; and their names are known from Iceland to Tarentum. The Convent of Erfurt, which produced Luther, is believed to have been a Celtic foundation, the last to survive in Germany; and at Milan, at St. Gall in Switzerland, and at Wurzburg, there may be seen manuscripts executed by men who had learned penmanship and theology in Iona or her daughter monasteries. The little island became supreme not only over the numerous monasteries created by her sons, but also over the senior foundations in Ireland. In the seventh century, she was at the height of her fame: the centre of a vast area of missionary activity, a renowned theological school, and a seat of learning.

Martyrdoms are all but unknown in the early history of the Celtic Church, and its saints are therefore not martyrs, but founders of churches and great teachers whose work and spirit survived and inspired those who came after them. Their names linger in many parts of Scotland. Loch Columcille in Skye, and the Isle of Inchcolm (Colum's Isle) in the Firth of Forth commemorate two of the many monasteries founded by Columba himself. The Cathedral of Aberdeen is dedicated to St. Machar, a successor of Drostan, who, along with Columba, converted a Pictish fort at Deer into a monastery, the centre of missionary

work in East Pictland. The name of the martyr
Donnan survives in Kildonan, of Blane of
Bute in Dunblane, of Mun in Kilmun, of Finnan
in Glenfinnan, of Maelrubha in Loch Maree.
Up and down the western seaboard and through-
out the isles are scattered the remains of little
Celtic chapels and monastic cells, built by
these holy men.

Comparatively little is known about the
system and theology of the Celtic Church
and the whole subject has given rise to much
controversy. Presbyterian, Episcopalian, and
Roman Catholic alike have claimed for their
particular communion affinity in doctrine or
usage with the Church of Columba. " The
striking fact ", says Troup, " is that they meet
round his memory." But while all modern
religious bodies may claim a share in the
spiritual inheritance of the ancient Church,
it is certain that none resembles it outwardly.

The Celtic Church was monastic in form.
Monasticism was probably first established
within the Christian Church by St. Basil, in
the East. In the fourth century, St. Jerome
introduced it into Western Europe, and St.
Martin of Tours into Gaul. Thence it was
brought by St. Ninian to Strathclyde, and a
little later by St. Patrick to Ireland. It was
the modified Irish form of monasticism — less
formalistic, and more vigorous and bracing

than that of the East—that Columba established in Iona. Its monasteries were not destined for recluses—though the church had its anchorites—but were rather religious settlements where men were fitted to go out into the world, and preach and minister to all and sundry. " The secret of the early Celts lay in this, that they linked sacrament with service, altar with hearth, worship with work."—(Troup.) Their active and enterprising spirit succeeded in creating the great missionary church that the times demanded.

Columba constituted his church on the model of the family, and the source of jurisdiction was vested in the Abbot. For over two hundred years after the Founder's death, the Abbot was chosen from his kin, in accordance with Irish tradition and clan feeling. In later days, when the clergy commonly married, hereditary succession was common also in benefices.

Diocesan episcopacy was unknown, but there were bishops of a sort. They appear to have been a very numerous body, appointed for the purpose of ordaining deacons and priests in their respective monasteries. In other respects, we gather, they lived the same life as the rest of the community, though honour was shown to the office.

Ordinations seem to have been irregular,

personal qualifications being deemed more
essential than ceremony. "More Scotico",
indeed, was used as a term of reproach
amongst the Roman Catholic clergy, who
exalted organization. "The Christian virtues
of humility and meekness," says Miss Ben-
tinck Smith, "in which the emissaries of the
British Church found Augustine deficient, were
valued in Iona above orthodoxy and correct-
ness of religious observance."

"It was a marked and distinctive feature
of the Iona system that while missionary
monks, North and South, willingly yielded
corporate obedience to Iona, and loyally owned
Columba's authority, they were always allowed
individual liberty and freedom of judgment."
—(Troup.) In later days, when great spiritual
leaders were lacking, this freedom tended to
degenerate into licence, and the loose organization of the Church led eventually, as we shall
see, to her corporate decay.

The precise nature of the doctrines of the
Celtic Church is not clearly known, but from
scattered allusions we gather that the scriptures
were the basis of teaching.

The monks appear to have enjoyed a very
liberal education. They were all bi-lingual
in Latin and Gaelic, and probably many were,
like Adamnan, proficient in Hebrew and Greek
as well. Within the monasteries, the services

were conducted in the Latin tongue, but the monks preached to the people in their native Gaelic. (To this day services are held in Iona in the ancient tongue.)

Not a few of the monks, in successive generations, were distinguished in poetry, rhetoric, general philosophy, and science (including astronomy). A love of the useful and fine arts was inculcated, and so highly was music valued that in the early days the faculty was regarded as a gift bestowed by heaven only on its favourites.

The work of the Celtic Church, south of the Border, is specially worthy of notice, for the evangelization of England is so generally accredited to St. Augustine—as in large measure it ought to be—that the share of Iona in the task is too apt to be overlooked.

St. Augustine landed in Kent shortly after Columba's death. One of his companions, Paulinus by name, came to Northumbria and made many converts, including King Edwin. Edwin, however, was slain in battle, and the new faith was discarded. Oswald, the heir to the throne, took refuge in Scotland, and received part of his education in Iona. On regaining his kingdom, his first care was to re-establish the Christian Church, and it was to Iona, not to Canterbury, that he turned for help. Aidan was sent, in 635, and he built a monastery, after

the Iona pattern, on the little island of Lindisfarne (Holy Island), off the east coast of Northumbria. He preached to the people, at first,
in his native Gaelic, while the king sat at his
feet, interpreting. Numbers of Scots missionaries followed Aidan, and Lindisfarne became a centre of missionary enterprise second
only to Iona. Aidan's successors, St. Finan
and St. Colman, added fresh lustre to the
southern monastery. Whitby, later the home
of Caedmon, was one of her daughter houses;
and so, too, was Melrose, which in turn produced
St. Cuthbert, the apostle of the Lothians, whose
name is borne by a famous church in Edinburgh.

St. Aidan and his followers not only restored
to Christianity areas that had lapsed since the
invasion of the Germanic tribes from which
our island race is mainly descended, but also
succeeded in winning over districts which
their predecessors had never been able to enter.
From the Celtic missionaries in the north and
from the Roman missionaries in the south,
there flowed two streams of missionary work
that eventually covered the whole land. " The
simplicity, the devotion, the free spirit, the
tenderness and love, the apostolic zeal of the
missionaries of Iona combined with the more
complete organization and the higher culture
of which Rome was the schoolmistress, to form

the English Church."—(Bishop Lightfoot of Durham.)

When, in due course, the Celtic and Roman missionaries came into contact, a controversy arose regarding the diversity of certain practices of the two churches: the tonsure, the celibacy of the clergy, and notably the date for the observance of Easter. In 463, Rome and the Continental churches had adopted a new method of calculating Easter Day, but the Celtic Churches in North Ireland and Scotland and the ancient British Church retained the old computation, which they believed to have been derived from the East, from the Apostle John himself. In 664, a counsel met at Whitby to settle these differences, and the king, who had hitherto favoured the Celtic Church observances, declared in favour of the Roman custom.[1]

[1] An old Gazetteer of Scotland gives a vigorous, if somewhat biased, account of this episode:—

"A celebrated, but very stupid dispute, at Whitby, in Yorkshire, between Colman, one of its alumni, and Wilfred, a Romanist, on the precious questions as to when Easter or the Passover should be celebrated, and with what kind of tonsure the hair of a professed religious should be cut, conducted on the one side by an appeal to the traditional authority of John the apostle, and on the other to the interpolated dictum of Peter, the alleged janitor of heaven, and supported on the part of Colman with all the zeal and influence of his Culdee brethren, ended, as it deserved to do, in the total discomfiture of the people of Iona, who totally forgot the moral dignity of their creed both by the jejuneness of the questions debated, and by the monstrous folly of appealing to the verdict of the Northumbrian Prince Oswi, a diademed ninny, who 'determined on no account to disregard the institutions of Peter who kept the keys of the kingdom of heaven'—this

This ended the supremacy of the Celtic Church in South Britain, and practically established there the Roman See.

The paschal question had previously estranged the Roman missionaries from the Welsh Christians, and was still to create dissension in North Britain. After Augustine reached England, Gregory wrote cautioning him against the rigorous enforcement of Roman usages, and advised him rather to choose from the customs of different churches those which seemed particularly suited to the place and the people. Augustine, however, gifted man as he was, lacked the tolerance and foresight of the great Pope, and while it is a matter of opinion whether or not he and his followers were wise in refusing to compromise in this particular issue, it is certain that they failed in dealing with the Celtic peoples, as others have since failed, because of " that passion for complete uniformity which has so frequently worked mischief in human affairs ".—(Rait.) Sheer tenacity of opinion, however, often overcomes a plastic temperament,

dispute gave a virtual death-blow to Culdeeism, and the influence of Icolmkill in England. . . . Under Adamnan, who died in 703, Iona proclaimed to the world its having commenced a career of apostacy . . . the ecclesiastics of the island put some trappings of finery upon their originally simple form of church government, they fraternized with the Romanists on the subject of keeping Easter . . . and though continuing to maintain the island's literary fame, very seriously defiled the essential purity of Christian faith and devotion."

and Adamnan, visiting Northumbria twenty-four years after the Synod of Whitby, did not fail to be moved by the rebuke of many learned ecclesiastics, that a small and obscure community like the Family of Hy should venture to defy the wisdom and might of Rome on so important an issue. The gentle, scholarly Abbot, who " shared the prevailing over-estimate of these things", returned to Iona—where, according to the old Irish chronicle, his appearance with the coronal tonsure of Rome in place of the Celtic half-shaven head was " a great surprise to his congregation "—and dutifully pointed out to the brethren the error of their ways. The brethren, however, refused to diverge from the ancient customs, and a schism was created, which persisted long after Adamnan's death. Meanwhile the Roman party grew steadily stronger, and in 717, Naiton, King of Picts, expelled from his kingdom all monks who refused to conform. One by one, Iona gave in on all the controversial points, and by 772, unity was restored within the Celtic Church.

VI

Later History

The Dim Eclipse

The first two centuries of the Celtic Church were the most glorious period in the history of Iona. "In later years", says Rait, "(the Church) did not escape the inevitable deterioration, and it had its reformers. . . . After the time of Columba, it seems to have had little influence in national affairs, but the persistence of its individual life indicates that it possessed a real hold upon the people of Scotland." Its best work was done as a missionary church; later, as civilization advanced, and the need of the times tended towards an organized religion, it was found lacking, and inevitably went down before the disciplined forces of Rome.

Hardly were its internal troubles over when a new danger threatened the Iona community from without. A series of invasions by Danish pirates is recorded: In 797, the island was pillaged; in 801–2, the monastery was burned to the ground; and in 806, Iona for the first time suffered " red martyrdom ", in the slaughter of sixty-eight monks, traditionally at Martyrs'

Bay. The afflicted monastery could no longer continue the oversight of the Church, and in 814, the primacy was transferred temporarily to Kells, in Ireland. The Iona monks, however, clung to their island, and bravely proceeded to build a new monastery, of stone, and on a better site, where the Abbey Church now stands. In 825, there was a second Danish massacre, the heathen bursting into the church one dark winter morning, during the celebration of Mass, and cutting down Blathmac, the acting superior, together with several of his monks. This is commemorated as the Passion of St. Blathmac and the Martyrs of Iona.

The primacy did not go back to Iona, but passed to Dunkeld, where Constantine, King of Picts, had erected a monastery far from the danger zone. Thence it passed to Abernethy, and finally, in 908, to St. Andrews. In Iona the office of Abbot was succeeded by that of Coarb of Columkill (Heir of Columba), held usually by the abbot of one of the greater Irish monasteries, who ruled Iona from afar. Thenceforward Iona, like the Celtic Church generally, steadily declined in importance.

Following the turbulent ninth century, there came a long period of relative peace, and henceforth there are many blanks in the history of Iona. The Danish invaders were succeeded by the Norse Vikings, but these were not aggressive towards the monastery. (The Danes, it may be said in fairness, are believed to have been incited to animosity against the Church because of the slaughter of their pagan kinsmen in North Germany by Charlemagne in the name of Christianity.)

In 980, a notable pilgrim, Anlaf, King of the Danes of Dublin, came to Iona after his defeat by the Irish, and spent his last days there in penance and good works. (Two centuries earlier, Neill Frassach, King of Ireland, and Artgal, King of Connaught, had died in Iona, having relinquished their thrones for the monastic life.) Six years later, the Danes once more descended on the island, and slaughtered the Abbot and fifteen monks, traditionally on the White Sands.

During the rest of the Celtic Church period, the possession of the Western Isles fluctuated between Scotland and Norway. In 1097, King Magnus of Norway (called Magnus Barelegs because of his adoption of the kilt during his long operations in the Hebrides) anchored his war-galleys in the Sound of Mull, and came ashore to do homage to the Isle of Columba.

Nothing more is heard of Iona for sixty-five years, when a notice appears in the Annals of Ulster of a deputation to Ireland in 1164.

In the meantime, Church affairs in Scotland had been practically revolutionized, mainly because of the marriage of Malcolm Canmore,

*The Sacristy
Doorway*

*The Choir
and Chancel*

son of Duncan, and successor to Macbeth on the Scottish throne, with Margaret, a Saxon princess, who, with her family, had taken refuge in Scotland after the Norman Conquest. [This marriage, indeed, marks the fall of Celtic and the rise of Anglian supremacy in Scotland, and the supersession at Court of the Gaelic tongue by " Scottis " or Scots, derived from the Anglian settlers in the Lothians.] Margaret, a thorough Saxon and devout member of the Roman Church, was genuinely distressed to find in the land of her adoption errors in the observance of Lent, neglect of the Sunday holy day, and " Masses in I know not what barbarous rite ". A woman of great piety and zeal, she " restored the monastery of Hy, which Columba, the servant of Christ, had erected in the time of Brude, son of Meilcon, King of Picts. It had fallen into ruin in the storms of war and the lapse of ages, but the faithful queen rebuilt and restored it, and gave the monks an endowment for the performance of the Lord's work " (Ordericus Vitalis).

But, though generous to Iona, Margaret set herself wholeheartedly to the task of Latinizing the Scottish Church. After a Celtic reaction, this policy was continued by her third son, David I, who abolished the Celtic liturgy, organized regular dioceses administered by bishops and parish priests, and replaced the Celtic monks and Culdees by Benedictine monks and Augustinian canons. By the end of his reign, practically all the mediæval sees had been founded.

The Culdees mentioned above were an order instituted in Dublin by St. Maelruain in 787.[1] The name is derived from the Celtic *Cele De*, the servant of God. They were hermits, leading a life of prayer and contemplation, and, by the ninth century, their cells were scattered over Scotland. Later, they fell away in many places from the old strict rules, and this served as an excuse for their suppression in the reform of the Scottish Church in the twelfth century.

Already, in 1093, succession in the old Celtic Church had come to an end, and though the religious life of Iona and the pilgrimages thither continued, a general decay of the Church was discernible. The twelfth century saw the complete Latinization of the National Church. Iona, owing to her isolated position, escaped the longest, but, early in the thirteenth century, Reginald, son and heir of the great Somerled, Lord of the Isles, established on the island a monastery of Benedictines, and, shortly afterwards, a community of nuns of the same order, " in honour of God and St. Columkill ".

In the last notice of Iona in the Irish Annals, it is related that in 1204 a monastery was erected

---

[1] The name Culdee is often erroneously applied to the clergy of the Celtic Church from the earliest times.

on the island by Cellach (presumably the first Abbot) " without any right, and in dishonour of the community ". On hearing of the calamity that had befallen the sacred isle, a party of incensed Derry men came over and pulled down the building. This seems to be an account, from the Irish point of view, of the appearance of the Benedictine community on Iona. After a tenure of approximately six and a half centuries, the Family of Hy, now far decayed, was ousted from its island sanctuary, and its remaining lands and churches were handed over to the usurpers. The fate of the monks is not known.

In the eleventh century, Iona had passed into the Diocese of Man and the Isles, which had been created by the Norwegian conquerors. In 1154, the See was put under the Archbishop of Trondjem, in Norway, and remained there until 1266, when, following the defeat of Haco of Norway at Largs three years earlier, the Hebrides were finally ceded to Scotland. Henceforth, Iona did homage to Dunkeld, once more the primatial See of Scotland.

The Benedictine occupation of Iona was uneventful. In 1203, Pope Innocent III's formal approval of the foundation of Iona Abbey was recorded in a letter of which a copy is preserved in the Vatican. In 1498, the Holy See was asked to erect the Abbacy into the

Bishopric of the Isles, and, by 1506, this was accomplished.

The light of Iona burned dimly, but steadily, through these dark and turbulent centuries, and, save for an incursion by Norwegian pirates in 1240, appears to have remained unscathed in the midst of " roving clans and savage barbarians ".

In 1549, Donald Monro, Dean of the Isles, visited the island, and from him we have a picture of Iona twelve years before the Reformation, when the community was swept into exile. " Within this ile ", he writes, " there is a monastery of mounckes, and ane uther of nuns, with a paroche-kirke, and sundrie uther chapells, dotat of auld by the Kings of Scotland and by Clandonald of the iyles."

Many precious manuscripts and books are said to have been carried off by the dispersed monks to the Scots monastery at Ratisbon and the Scots colleges at Douay and Rome, but none of these has been identified.

There is no evidence that any systematic attempt to destroy the buildings was made at the time of the Reformation in 1560, when the island and the lands formerly belonging to the monastery passed into the hands of Maclean of Duart.

In 1609, Andrew Knox, who was made Bishop of the Isles in the temporary episcopate estab-

lished a year later, held a convention of several
chiefs of the Highlands and islands, on Iona.
Here the " Statutes of Icolmkill " were drawn
up and subscribed, the chiefs pledging themselves to repair the churches throughout their
territories, to provide parish ministers, to pro-
mote the observance of the Sabbath day, and
to endeavour to put a stop to certain undesir-
able practices which were then prevalent.

In 1617, the Abbey of Iona was annexed
to the Bishopric of the Isles. Eighteen years
later, Charles I wrote to Maclean of Duart
asking him to restore the Island of Icolmkill
to the Bishop, and in the same year ordered
the Lords of the Exchequer to pay to the
Bishop the sum of £400 for the restoration
of the Abbey Church; but this grant was never
made, owing, doubtless, to the troubles of the
time; for when Sacheverell, Governor of Man,
visited Iona in 1688, the buildings were in ruins.
" Though they have no minister," he tells us,
" they constantly assemble in the great church
on Sundays, where they spend most of the day
in private devotions."

In 1693, Iona passed from the Macleans to
the Campbells, and it still remains in the hands
of their chief, the Duke of Argyll.

In 1899, the Abbey Church and other ecclesiastical buildings on the island were gifted by
the eighth Duke to the Church of Scotland.

The island life continues its even tenor.
The nettle still " sheds her snows above kings'
heads ", and the thistle " waves where bishops'
mitres stood ", but the " long sleep " which
fell upon the island is now at an end, and there
is a general stirring. The Abbey Church is
once more a place of worship, and in 1894,
an Episcopal chapel was consecrated in the
newly built " St. Columba's House "—known
locally as the Bishop's House—which was used
for a time as a house of retreat for clergy of
that body. A library, founded a century ago, and
continually added to, is housed in the island.
In a studio in the village, the old Celtic designs
in which the island is so rich are reproduced
in beautiful articles of wood, brass, and other
materials, and notably in Iona silver jewellery.

After the World War of 1914–1918, the well-
known Gaelic scholar, Mr. Angus Robertson,
set on foot a scheme for the establishment of a
Gaelic College on the island. The plan is
sponsored by a number of American business
men, many of them Scots by descent, with
others who believe that in our ancient Gaelic
culture, with its more human and at the same
time more spiritual values, lies an antidote for
the ills wrought by our modern materialistic
civilization. The College has not yet mate-
rialized, nor does it now seem likely that if and
when it does it will be situated in Iona.

Meanwhile, another movement has taken shape and rooted itself in the island. This is the Iona Community, established in 1938 by the Reverend George F. Macleod. The Community, which in 1950 was integrated by the General Assembly of the Church of Scotland into the life of the Church, believes that " mankind's primary problem is how to plan society and at the same time preserve the rights of the individual. In the Christian Church—provided she can be wed again to ' the common life '—lies the only key to the world problem." In this belief, the members of the Community, during the summer months when they are resident on the island, consider these and cognate matters and in particular how, in parish organization and practices of worship, the Church can most adequately serve the present age. An integral part of the work is the rebuilding of the ruined parts of the Abbey—a common act of labour against the background of which the various problems are discussed.

In the winter months, during their period of membership of the Community (normally two years), ministers work in pairs within the parish system of the Church of Scotland, each pair under the supervision of a parish minister. Thereafter they become absorbed in the normal ministry.

VII

The Antiquities

Few of the many ecclesiastical ruins in Iona to-day are older than the early thirteenth century. The cursory visitor will probably limit his attention to the mediæval ruins, which include the Cathedral—the most impressive and interesting of the remains—the Monastery, the Nunnery, and St. Oran's Chapel; the ancient burial-ground of Reilig Odhrain; and the Crosses and sculptured stones. For those with leisure and interest there is much else.

MACLEAN'S CROSS. On the road from the village to the Cathedral, on the spot, it is said, where Columba rested half-way on the last day of his life, there stands a mediæval, way-side cross, carved from a thin slab of schist, ten feet high above its pedestal. On its western side, the central figure is a crucified Christ in a long robe; a fleur-de-lis is above, and a chalice is on one side. The shaft is ornamented with foliage and the interlacing that is characteristic of Celtic ornament. The east

St. John's Cross

St. Martin's Cross

side has an ornamental pattern, and below are two animals and a mounted knight with helmet and lance. The cross is believed to be fifteenth-century work, and probably commemorates a Maclean of Duart—that branch of the clan in whose country Iona lay.

THE ABBEY CHURCH, which is dedicated to the Virgin, stands on the site of a church erected by Reginald Macdonald in 1203. Originally an Abbey, in 1507 it became the Cathedral of the Diocese of the Isles, which it remained until the Reformation. The building is cruciform, measuring 148 feet 7 inches from east to west, and 70 feet 3 inches from north to south, with a massive square tower 70 feet high. Though there are traces of late Norman, most of the building dates from the late fifteenth and early sixteenth century. The circular pier-arch, as Ferguson points out, " is used with the mouldings of the thirteenth century, and the pointed arch is placed on a capital of intertwined dragons, more worthy of a Runic cross or tombstone than a Gothic edifice. The tower windows are filled with quatrefoil tracery, in a manner very unusual, and a mode of construction adopted which does not perhaps exist anywhere else in Britain."

Other details of interest within the building are the capitals of the tower piers and of the pillars, which are carved with a curious medley of subjects: foliage, grotesque monsters, groups of men and beasts, and Biblical subjects; the carved Gothic sedilia; the tombs of two fifteenth-century abbots of Iona, John Mackinnon and Kenneth Mackenzie, north and south of the sanctuary; a stone with an incised Celtic cross, which, according to tradition, was St. Columba's pillow and later his gravestone (for Adamnan says they set up his stone pillow as a monument at his grave), and some sculptured stones brought in from Reilig Odhrain for their better preservation. There are also two modern tombs—those of the eighth Duke and Duchess of Argyll.

COLUMBA'S TOMB. On the north side of the entrance to the nave of the Church is a small and very ancient oratory, the east end of which is formed by the cloister wall. It contains two stone cists, of which the greater, on the south side, traditionally held the shrine of Columba, and the lesser, that on the north, possibly that of his faithful attendant Diormit, or, as some think, of St. Blathmac, who was killed in the Danish raid of 825.

From the time of the first Danish raids on Iona, the shrine was freely translated between Ireland and Scotland (including Dunkeld), and was lost sight of before the Benedictine settlement.

ST. MARTIN'S CROSS. A few yards from Columba's tomb, and directly facing it, stands the great Cross of Iona, dedicated to St. Martin of Tours, a friend of St. Ninian and contemporary of St. Patrick, and one of the most outstanding figures of the fourth century. The cross, now hoary with years, is of massive schist on a granite pedestal. On the east side it is decorated with bosses and serpents; on the west, the central subject is a Virgin and Child surrounded by four angels, and on the arms and shafts are animals and groups of human figures, portraying scriptural subjects, with bosses and serpents below. The cross is of the Celtic period, probably tenth century, and alone of its contemporaries has weathered the ages. The broken shafts of two possibly earlier crosses—St. John's and, to the south, St. Matthew's—stand between St. Martin's Cross and the oratory.

THE BLACK STONES OF IONA. Near St. Columba's Tomb there stood formerly one of the most ancient and sacred of Iona's relics—the Black Stones of Iona, so called, not from their colour, but from the black doom that fell on any who dared to violate an oath sworn upon them. So recently as the reign of James VI and I, two clans who had spent centuries in bloody feud met here and solemnly pledged themselves to friendship. The last of these stones disappeared about a century ago.

There is a tradition that the Coronation Stone in Westminster Abbey was originally one of the famous Black Stones. Its legendary history is very ancient, for it is believed to have been reverenced as Jacob's pillow by the tribes who brought it from the East in the first wave of Celtic emigration. "On this stone—the old Druidic Stone of Destiny, sacred among the Gael before Christ was born—Columba crowned Aidan King of Argyll. Later the stone was taken to Dunstaffnage, where the Lords of the Isles were made princes: thence to Scone, where the last of the Celtic Kings of Scotland was crowned on it. It now lies in Westminster Abbey, a part of the Coronation Chair, and since Edward I every British monarch has been crowned upon it. If ever the Stone of Destiny be moved again, that writing on the wall will be the signature of a falling dynasty."—(Fiona Macleod.)

Skene questions all its history before its use for Scottish coronations at Scone.

THE MONASTERY. The partially restored Benedictine monastery, founded by Reginald, Lord of the Isles, in the early thirteenth century, adjoins the Abbey Church on the north. There is a square cloister, which has the Church nave on the south, the chapter-house on the east, and the refectory on the north. A room above the chapter-house is believed to have housed the famous Library of Iona. The kitchen stands a little apart, north of the refectory. A kitchen midden, containing bones, shells, and other refuse, was discovered between the two buildings a few years ago.

TRACES OF CELTIC MONASTERY. The first simple, monastic buildings in Iona were erected by Columba, thirteen hundred years ago, and probably several buildings have arisen and decayed between that date and the foundation of the last Celtic monastery. We know that the wooden buildings burned by the Danes in 802 were succeeded by a building of stone, but it is hardly likely that the present remains are those of the first, or even the second, stone monastery.

The Celtic monastery consisted ordinarily of a group of small stone churches of simple design and peculiar orientation, dominated by a round tower which served as belfry, lookout station, and place of refuge. Services were held in the little churches simultaneously; or sometimes successively, so that a continuous round of praise was kept up, day and night.

The traces of such a monastery in Iona

include a small, roofless church, 33 feet by 16, north-east of the Monastery buildings; the foundation of a round tower (discovered in 1908); the traces of what seem to have been cells; and the remains of an outer wall of a range of buildings west of the cloister. " There seems to have been a central community house, having, on the east, the small church and other detached buildings, whose remains are visible, and, on the west, the round tower and high crosses contiguous to the little oratory of the shrine. There were outlying chapels also, for St. Mary's, St. Oran's, St. Kenneth's, St. Ronan's, and Cladh an Diseirt are Celtic sites." —(Trenholme.)

THE NUNNERY. Like the Monastery, the Nunnery was established at the beginning of the thirteenth century by Reginald, Lord of the Isles, whose sister Bethog, or Beatrice, was the first Abbess of Icolmkill. The early nuns were Benedictines; later—the date and the reason are unknown—they changed to the Augustine order.

The architecture is Norman, of a type commonly used prior to the twelfth century. The apartments grouped around the enclosure include a chapter-house with stone seats, a chapel with an aisle on the north side, a refectory and a kitchen on the south. In 1923, the buildings were repaired and the garden in the cloister garth planted by her family in memory of Mrs. R. J. Spencer. There are several sculptured tombstones within the walls, the most notable being that of the Prioress Anna (*ob.* 1543)—an effigy in low relief—and the beautiful Nunnery Cross.

Sacheverell, who visited Iona in 1688, tells us that the Nunnery chapel was the burial-place of all the ladies in that part of Scotland, as St. Oran's was of the men of rank and distinction; and it continued so till the end of the eighteenth century.

On the north side of the nunnery stand the ruins of St. Ronan's Church, which appears to have been the parish church before the Reformation.

REILIG ODHRAIN. The ancient burying-ground of Reilig Odhrain lies, " weel biggit about with staine and lyme ", a little south-west of the Abbey Church. The name signifies the burial-place of Oran. According to a tale in the *Old Irish Life of Columba*, it was revealed to the saint that a human sacrifice would be necessary for the success of his mission. His brother Oran, one of the twelve brethren who accompanied him to Iona, offered himself, and was buried alive. On the third day, Columba caused the grave to be opened, where-

upon Oran opened his eyes, and said: " Death
is no wonder, nor is hell as it is said." Such
heresy was not pleasing to the saint's ear, and
his reply, " Earth, earth on Oran's eye, lest
he further blab ", has passed into a proverb.

This story is not mentioned by Adamnan,
nor is the name Oran to be found in the list
of Columba's twelve companions. The name
may have been derived from one Oran, whose
death is recorded fifteen years before the land-
ing of Columba, or from a monk of the same
name, whose burial may have been the first
in the community. Reilig Odhrain was probably
the original burial-place of the Family of Hy,
for Columba is believed to have been buried
here (though his remains were enshrined at a
later period, and placed in the little oratory, as
afore described), and, on this account, Reilig
Odhrain became a famous sanctuary for fugitives.

Within this " awful ground ", as Dr. Johnson describes it, lie the surviving gravestones
of the dead of thirteen centuries. When Iona
was at the zenith of her fame and had become
a holy place in all the land, the bodies of princes,
chiefs, and ecclesiastics throughout Celtic Scotland and beyond it were brought here for
burial. An ancient prophecy may have in-
creased the desire for interment in Iona:—

> " Seven years before the judgment,
> The sea shall sweep over Erin at one tide,

*Piscina and Sedelia, St. Columba Pillow (in metal case)
and Effigy of Abbot Mackenzie*

The Ridge of The Chiefs

And over blue-green Isla;
But I of Colum of the Church shall swim ".

Records of royal burials are found in the
old *Chronicle of the Picts and Scots*, from
Adamnan's time onwards. Kenneth Mac-
alpine, the first king of a united Scotland, was
buried here in 860, and the precedent was
followed by most of the kings after him for
two centuries. Shakespeare's lines may be
recalled:

Rosse. Where is Duncan's body ?
Macduff.   Carried to Columskill,
   The sacred storehouse of his predecessors,
   And guardian of their bones.

Macbeth, too, was laid to rest here, beside his
reputed victim.

Duncan's son, Malcolm Canmore, was the
first to break the tradition of Royal burials in
Iona; his body lies in Dunfermline.

The remains of sixty kings in all are believed
to lie " eirded in this very fair kirkyaird ".
Monro, Dean of the Isles, who visited the island
in 1549, describes three tombs, resembling
small chapels, and bearing the legends " Tumulus Regum Scotiae ", " Tumulus Regum Hiber-
niae ", and " Tumulus Regum Norwegiae ",
respectively. Here were interred forty-eight
crowned kings of Scotland, four of Ireland,
and seven of Norway. When Pennant visited

the island in 1772, the tombs were in ruins, and the inscriptions lost.

Most of the older tombstones have been gathered together in two parallel rows, near the middle of the enclosure. The Ridge of the Kings lies to the west; the Ridge of the Chiefs to the east.

The RIDGE OF THE KINGS contains twenty-one stones, which are unnamed, save the following, numbered from left to right:—

3. Bishop *Aodh Cama-chasach* (Hugh of the Crooked Legs).

12. Reginald, Lord of the Isles (*ob.* 1207), founder of the Benedictine Monastery and Nunnery on Iona.

The RIDGE OF THE CHIEFS, called also the Ridge of the Macleans, contains nineteen stones, of which again many are nameless.

4. A Macleod of Lewis (*ob. circa* 1532).

5. Called " The Rider ", from the figure of a mounted knight with spear at charge, at the top of the stone. A fourteenth-century Maclean.

8. A Maclean, known as Ailean nan Sop (Allan of the Straw), a noted pirate and free-booter in his youth, whose by-name is derived from the combustible with which he freely set fire to houses during his raids.

14. " The Four Priors." A stone with four panels, commemorating four Iona ecclesiastics of the fifteenth century.

15. Maclean of Lochbuie (*circa* 1500).

16. Maclean of Coll.

17. Another Maclean of Lochbuie, *Eoghan a' Chinn Bhig* (Ewan of the Little Head), who was killed in a fierce clan fight about 1538. " It was a common belief in the olden time that this personage always appeared when a member of his family was about to die. A little over fifty years ago, a native of the island declared that he saw Ioin pass him at Maclean's Cross on his black horse, with his little head under his arm."—(Macmillan).

19. Dr. John Beton (*ob.* 1657). According to Skene, the Betons, or Macbeths, were hereditary physicians in Isla and Mull, and also sennachies (historians) of the Macleans.

On the eastern side of the Ridge of the Kings there lies a rough block of red granite, bearing an incised cross, and believed to mark the grave of a nameless king of France.

Near the western wall of the graveyard there is a stone erected by the Government of the United States to the memory of sixteen persons who went down with the American ship *Guy Mannering*, off the west coast of Iona on New Year's Eve, 1865.

St. Oran's Chapel. Within Reilig Odhrain is a small, roofless chapel, 29 feet by 15 in dimension and dedicated to St. Oran. It

is the oldest of the mediæval ruins, and is
believed to have been erected by the pious
Margaret, the Saxon queen of Malcolm Canmore, in the eleventh century. The doorway
has a richly carved Norman arch of later date
than the chapel itself, and a mediæval altar-
tomb, surmounted by a triple arch, has been
built into the southern wall. The chapel has
been recently repaired.

CLACH BRÀTH. Near the edge of the path
leading to St. Oran's Chapel, there lies a
broad, flat stone, with a slit and cavity on
its surface. Here there used to lie some small,
round stones which pilgrims were wont to
turn sunwise within the cavity; for it was
commonly believed that the " bràth ", or end
of the world, would not arrive until this stone
should be worn through.

THE SCULPTURED STONES. One of the
many names of antiquity by which Iona has
been called is *Innis nan Druineach*, the Island
of Cunning Workmen, or, more freely translated, of the Sculptors. Iona was a centre not
only of Celtic religion and Celtic learning
but also of Celtic art. The Celtic race in these
islands achieved nothing—indeed attempted
nothing—in the higher planes of sculpture or
painting; for these were the Dark Ages, when
Greece had passed into obscurity, and the

Renaissance was yet to come. The artistic genius of the Gael was confined to decorative art, but within that domain reached a rare degree of excellence.[1]

Celtic art in Scotland is almost entirely Christian. In the early days, parchment was the sole medium of expression, and the monks of Iona were devoted to the copying of manuscripts. Columba, as we know, was a skilled scribe, and so was Baithne, his cousin and successor. There still survive some priceless examples of this "abstract and unemotional art", such as the Book of Kells, an eighth-century Iona manuscript (now in Dublin) which is unrivalled in its sensitive beauty of line and colour. When, at a later date, stone came into use, there were shown the same qualities that characterize the illuminated work —purity, delicacy, and exquisite workmanship.

The sculptured stones are distributed variously. Some are sheltered within the Abbey

[1] The Celtic races have been necessarily almost impotent in the higher branches of the plastic arts. . . . The abstract, severe character of the Druidical religion, its dealing with the eye of the mind rather than the eye of the body, its having no elaborate temples and beautiful idols, all point this way from the first; its sentiments cannot satisfy itself, cannot even find a resting-place for itself in colour and form ; it presses on to the impalpable, the ideal. The forest of trees and the forest of rocks, not hewn timber and carved stones, suit its aspirations for something not to be bounded or expressed. . . . Ireland, that has produced so many powerful spirits, has produced no great sculptors or painters (Matthew Arnold : *Study of Celtic Literature*).

Church, and some—including St. Martin's Cross
and a few broken cross-shafts—are in the Church
precincts. Others are in Reilig Odhrain—in
the Ridges of the Kings and Chiefs—and in
St. Oran's Chapel. The women's memorial
stones are gathered within the Nunnery. Maclean's Cross stands apart, on the roadside, not
far from the Nunnery ruins.

Two distinct periods are represented in the
workmanship of the stones: the earlier are of
the pure Celtic type, while the later, or mediæval ones, show alien influences. The latter
naturally predominate.

There are roughly three types of stone.

The first category includes a few unshaped
boulders, with incised crosses, all probably
of early date. The most celebrated is the traditional pillow of Columba, now preserved
in the Abbey Church.

Secondly, there are numerous grave-slabs.
The flat stones, with crosses incised or in relief,
belong to the Celtic period. A few are probably early specimens, but those bearing inscriptions are considered from the style of
lettering to belong to near the end of the Celtic
Church period. The Irish Cross (St. Oran's
Chapel) and the Nunnery Cross (Nunnery) are
two fine specimens of this period.

The flat slabs of the mediæval period are
more ornate than the earlier ones. Foliage

decoration is used, and sometimes the figures of animals. Many bear emblems, such as the warrior's claymore, the abbot's crozier, the chief's galley (that of each island clan was distinctive), the Cross, or the triquetra (Celtic emblem of the Trinity). On the women's stones such emblems as shears, mirrors, and combs appear.

The gravestones include also some recumbent effigies, all mediæval work.

Thirdly, there are the high standing crosses of both Celtic and mediæval periods. These crosses are believed to have been numerous at one time: there is a tradition, indeed, though it is far from reliable, that no less than three hundred and fifty of them were flung into the sea at the time of the Reformation.

The Celtic Cross is distinguished from all others by its form, which combines two symbols, the ring and the cross, the ring intersecting the arms and shaft of the cross. The decorative treatment is also distinctive, and it is noteworthy that in the two hundred and fifty crosses of the Irish Church, no crucifixion is found.

Only two crosses remain intact in Iona: the splendid St. Martin's, already described, which is of the purest Celtic type; and Maclean's, which, though Celtic in form, is stamped mediæval by its foliage decoration and its central figure of Christ crucified.

VIII

Topography

By far the greater number of visitors to Iona spend only a few hours on the island, and as a rule their time is fully occupied in the inspection of the antiquities described in the previous chapter. Full of interest as these are, people whose attention is thus confined are apt to carry away an impression not so much of the Iona of Columba as of the mediæval Iona, in the relatively uneventful era of the Benedictine occupation. " It is rather the fair sea-beauty and imaginative charm of the place that links us with the ancient, simple days of material poverty and spiritual fruitfulness ", says Trenholme; and in order to get at this Iona, it is essential to make a stay on the island. This is not a difficult matter, for there are two comfortable inns, of a character harmonious with their surroundings, and most of the cottages make provision for visitors. A few houses, in addition, are to let for the summer months.

This chapter is specially intended for those

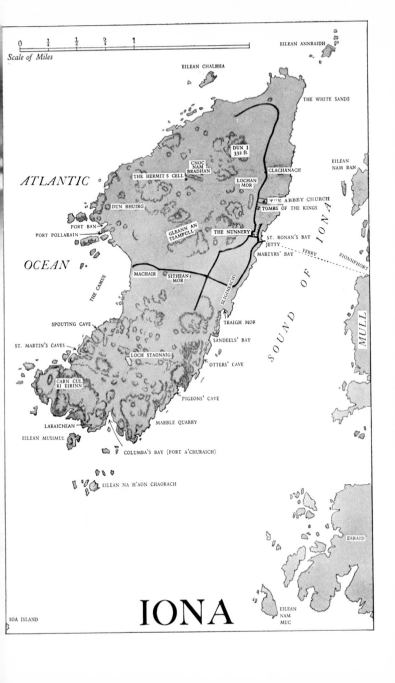

IONA

who have leisure to appreciate the manifold attractions of the little island. It is not within the compass of a small handbook to deal in a detailed way with even the history and antiquities of the island, much less its geology, natural history, and other aspects. The specialist will have recourse to the standard authorities, and for others who desire to extend their knowledge in any particular aspect, a small bibliography is appended.

With leisure, the imaginative will be able to linger in the quiet places beloved of Columba and his followers, and to spirit themselves into the dim past; the artist will discover the beauty of the atmospheric effects; the antiquarian will find fresh fields of interest; the nature-lover will be absorbed in the varieties of bird, and flower, and stone; the rambler can wander at will over moorland and rock and sheeny sand; and many pleasing trips can be made to the entrancing islets that surround Iona.

In this chapter, the places of special interest in Iona will be enumerated and briefly annotated. Beginning just north of the Abbey Church, the route followed will run roughly in a counter-sunwise direction.

SITE OF COLUMBA'S MONASTERY. From a piecing of evidence (see Trenholme: *Story of*

Iona) it had been determined that the tract of ground lying immediately to the north of the Church, and inclining to the seashore, with the Lochan Mor on the west, the mill-stream on the south, and the stone Blathnat probably indicating its northern extremity, was the site of the monastery erected by Columba, over thirteen hundred years ago.

As the result of excavations carried out in the summers of 1956 and 1957 by a team of archeologists representing several Universities, the Columban foundation can now be partially reconstructed, at any rate on paper. It was defined by a *vallum*, a high bank with an outer ditch, roughly rectangular in shape and some 1100 by 500 feet inside. Its traces can be seen clearly on the high ground west of Tor Abb, running along by the football ground and then curving round in the field north of the Abbey block. Here, "it has been picked up, partly from aerial photographs, partly by a method of electrical surveying, and partly by close examination in favourable light. It runs back more or less under the recently re-built Abbot's House, and then probably along the east pavement of the Cloisters. We must assume that it goes below the present Abbey, and curves back to the west roughly where the south transept lies. Between here and the gate, the ditch was finally located, at a depth of some six feet, in a system of rectangular trenches sunk on the south side of the Abbey this year (1957)." [1]

Within this enclosure the brethren, many of whose names are preserved in Adamnan's *Life*, lived, performed manual labour, illuminated precious manuscripts, prayed, meditated and died. The settlement is believed to have been quite small, consisting of perhaps a dozen huts, the offices, and the little church that formed the focus. It appears to have been situated close to the west wall of the enclosure, approximately where the Abbot's House, the cloister garth, the refectory and the western half of the Abbey now stand. Earlier in the century, foundations of small round cells were found on the west side of the cloister garth, and it is hoped to re-open these.

St. Columba's Cell. The Saint's private cell stood a little apart from the centre of monastic life. The clues given in Adamnan all point to Tor Abb, but the exact spot remained a matter of speculation until the summer of 1957, when the summit was stripped and a cell revealed that conforms to all the evidence we have. It lay beneath a ridge " like a cow's backbone ", and its low stone walls, " carefully keyed into irregularities in the living rock," and no more than a few feet high, were surmounted by stubs of small wooden stakes, in the form of charcoal. This suggested a kind of wigwam

[1] *The Coracle*, November, 1957.

construction of wood, turf, heather and thatch for the roof. Within the cell was a broad slab of rock that could serve as a seat or bed. "*Pro stramine nudam petram, et pro pulvillo lapidem*," wrote Adamnan of Columba—for mattress the bare rock, and for pillow a stone. In so far as the archeologists will commit themselves without positive evidence, and unless evidence to the contrary is ever brought to light, this will be accepted as the veritable cell of the Saint.

THE LOCHAN MÓR (the Great Pond), now drained to a bog, was originally the monastery mill-pond, and from it the MILL-STREAM still trickles along its deep bed just north of the Abbey Church to the shore. Adamnan mentions a kiln and a granary in the proximity of the monastery, and Pennant in 1772 saw by the mill-stream "the ruins of a kiln" (for drying corn) "and a granary; and near it was the mill." Traces of buildings still remain on the high road by the mill-stream, west of the road.

IOMAIR AN ACHD (Ridge of the Act). A little north of Clachanach, immediately east of the road, and almost obliterated by it, there is a mound where, according to local tradition, the monks used to meet in council. "Perhaps", says Trenholme, "the convention of the elders sat there who chose St. Aidan from their number for the English mission, in the

The Village

End of the Pilgrim Road through Mull to Iona

year 635, as described by the Venerable Bede."
Such council hills were a feature of the Celtic
and Scandinavian civilization of these times.

THE STONE BLATHNAT. Midway between
the Ridge of the Act and the seashore, there
lies a great flat boulder — 27 feet by 18 — of
red granite, now grey with lichen. This stone
is a relic of the great ice age, but it has an
additional interest. An eleventh-century scribe,
in a preface to Columba's great hymn: " Altus
Prosator ", speaks of " a certain stone that was
in the monastery, Blathnat its name, and it still
exists, and upon it division is made in the refectory ". According to another scribe, " luck
was left upon all the food that was put thereon ".
There is every reason to identify the great
boulder with the stone of the old Irish docu-
ments, and it therefore marks the site of the
refectory, which was probably built over it.

CLADH AN DISEIRT (Burial - ground of the
Hermitage) or CLADH IAIN (St. John's Cemetery). In a lonely spot a little south - west
of the stone Blathnat are two rough granite
pillars, which, with a third stone that lay across
the top, formed a rude gateway to what was
formerly a small enclosure. In 1880, excavators
discovered here the foundation of a hermit's
cell of the oblong type, 26 feet by 17, facing
due east, and having traces of an altar-piece at

the east end. These " disarts " or hermitages were built sometimes in solitary places, sometimes in the neighbourhood of a monastery. The hermits spent their time chiefly in prayer and contemplation, and were frequently sought as spiritual advisers. They studied also, and worked at handicrafts, like other monks.

A hermit was usually buried in or near his cell: hence the name of the ground adjoining this disart.

THE CAUSEWAY (*Iomair an Tàchair*, Ridge of the Gleaning), or BISHOP'S WALK, is an ancient roadway, 22 feet wide and 220 yards long, built high above the Lochan Mór. Skene suggests that it was constructed by Cillene Droiteach (Cillen the Bridgemaker), the fourteenth Abbot, as a means of communication between the monastery and the Hermit's Cell in the wild, north-west tract of the island. Traces of a roadway connecting the Causeway and the Cell are still to be seen.

THE HERMIT'S CELL lies deep in turf and heather, a few yards south-west of Cnoc nam Bradhan (Hill of the Querns). Only the foundation, on which stones have been piled, is left. It is almost circular in shape, and about 18 feet in diameter. The Gaelic name, *Cobhain Cuildich*, is popularly translated Culdee Cell, but this *carcair*—so the Irish call the beehive hut of a hermit—is probably of much greater antiquity than the Culdee order. It is possible that the above-mentioned Cillen, who was an anchorite abbot, ruled the monastery from this spot, and Skene thinks that it may have been originally one of Columba's prayer places. " Its position looking out over the ocean to Tiree ", says Trenholme, " suits Adamnan's description of the place among the bushes, remote from men, and meet for prayer, where Columba went to pray one day and beheld (perhaps in a storm of thunder and lightning) hosts of demons fighting with darts in the sky, above Iona, but at last driven off to Tiree."

Traces of a walled walk, ascending to and enclosing the hillock, are mentioned in the *Statistical Account* published a hundred years ago, but the last vestiges seem to have disappeared.

WELL OF THE NORTH WIND (*Tobair na Gaoithe Tuath*). This is one of the magic wells of antiquity. It lies north of Cnoc nam Bradhan, not far from the Hermit's Cell. Here, in olden times, sailors and others brought offerings to charm up a wind from the north. A well of the south wind traditionally exists in Iona, but can no longer be traced.

DÙN-I (Hill, or Hill-Fortress of I), the one hill of Iona, lies immediately behind the Abbey

Church. Ascent can be made from any side, but the best route from the village ascends just behind Clachanach. There is an old superstition that good luck follows those who have made the ascent seven times. A cairn marks the summit, where possibly an island fortress once stood.

On a clear day, a vast expanse of hill and sea and sky is revealed, and a sunset or, better, a sunrise seen from Dùn-I is a thing not to be forgotten. The principal islands within sight of the summit are enumerated in the first chapter, and in the last there is quoted an impression of Iona from the slopes of Dùn-I, by Fiona Macleod.

THE WELL OF YOUTH or POOL OF HEALING (*Tobair na h'Aoise*, Well of the Age). On the northern brow of Dùn-I, half hidden by an over-hanging rock, there lies a small triangular pool, the fame of which used to be far spread. Here, through ages past, pilgrims of each generation have lingered at the enchanted hour of dawn, " to touch the healing water the moment the first sun-ray quickens it ". So they thought to recover their lost youth: some, perhaps, its physical strength and beauty; others its dreams and aspirations.

THE WHITE SANDS skirt the north-western shore. They are of unusual whiteness, and are composed of the powdered shells of innumerable land-snails. The stretch of sand known as *Tràigh Bhàn nam Manach* (White Strand of the Monks) is believed to have been the scene of the third slaughter of Iona monks by the Danes, and the dark, steep rock at the northern extremity is said to have been stained with the blood of the victims.

Dùn Bhuirg (Hill of the Fort) has traces of what looks like fortification. The foundation of a hermit's cell similar to the one at Cnoc nam Bradhan lies in a hollow a little south-east of the hillock.

Gleann an Teampuill (Glen of the Church) lies about the middle of the island, north of the Machair. It is believed to be the site of the monastery previously mentioned, which was erected by the Benedictine monks on their taking possession of Iona, and intended, Skene thinks, for the Celtic monks, that they might be out of the way. There was an old burial-ground at the head of the glen, but no traces of it remain.

The Machair (*A' Mhachair*, the Plain) is a tract of arable land in the middle west of the island. Adamnan speaks of Columba's monks as labouring here at the harvest, and it was to this spot that Columba was driven in a cart to tell the brethren of his approaching end.

THE CAMUS is the name of the long, curving bay that skirts the Machair. Hither it was that Columba sent a monk to tend the wounded crane alighted from Ireland. It has one or two sheltered, sandy inlets that are specially suited for bathing. Poll-eirinn (Pool of Ireland), at the north end of the bay, is believed to have been in later times a smugglers' landing-place.

ANGELS' HILL (in Gaelic *Cnoc nan Aingeal*, but better known locally by its old Gaelic name *Sithean Mór*, great fairy-mound) is a grassy knoll just south of the extremity of the road leading to the Machair. As its ancient name signifies, it is one of the fairy knolls of pre-Christian times, one of several in Iona. In these knolls, they say, the Wee Folk were wont to hold revel, and mortals passing by have heard faint strains of fairy music proceeding from within. But the Angels' Hill has also a special association with Columba; for one day—so Adamnan relates—the saint was seen by a prying monk to ascend this hillock, and as he stood " praying with hands spread out to heaven; and raising his eyes heavenward, behold! suddenly a marvellous thing appeared,

. . . for Holy Angels, citizens of the Celestial
Country, clad in white garments, came flying
to him with wonderful speed, and stood round
the holy man as he prayed; and after some con-
versation with the blessed man, that heavenly
band . . . sped swiftly back to the high
heavens ".

The prying monk stood probably on the
adjacent mound called Cnoc Odhrain, beside
the croft of that name.

In later days, according to Pennant, the
Angels' Hill was the scene of a general cavalcade
at the Feast of St. Michael, the natives coursing
round the hillock on horseback—a ceremony
common throughout the Western Isles; for,
says Trenholme, " Michael of the Snow-white
Steeds appears with Mary Mother and Kind
Columkill in the old songs and hymns of the
Islesmen, as a great protector by sea and shore ".

THE SPOUTING CAVE. A little south of the
Machair is a dark cavern into which the sea
enters by a natural tunnel at the base of the
rocks, and from which, finding itself trapped, it
seeks escape through a cleft or " blow-hole "
in the roof, driving a column of water high above
the cliffs. The action can best be seen at high
tide, with the wind in the south-west.

CARN CUL RI EIRINN (*The Cairn of-the-Back-*

to-Erin) stands on *Druim an Aoinidh* (Ridge of the Cliff) near the south-western extremity of the island. This cairn is believed to mark the spot where Columba scanned the horizon on his arrival, in order to be assured that his beloved Erin was out of sight. Among the many poems attributed to Columba, there is one of great beauty that remarkably describes the scene from this spot.

PORT LARAICHEAN (Bay of Ruins) lies near the middle of the southern shore, opposite Eilean Musimul. A little back from the beach, on a grassy terrace of artificial construction, are the foundations of six or seven circular stone huts, with a larger and squarer one on a rock near by. These, according to Dr. Reeves, are traces of by far the oldest buildings on the island. Sheltered all around by high rocks, save where it looks out on to the sea, " the hamlet could be well defended with bows and arrows, but whether it was the home of Picts or Scots who lived before Columba, or of later monks or hermits, is unknown " (Trenholme).

GARADH EACHAINN OIG (Garden of Young Hector)—the name probably commemorates a Maclean of Duart—at the head of Port na Curaich, and PORT GOIRTEIN IOMHAIR (Bay of

Ivor's Garth), farther east, have both traces of little buildings.

PORT A' CHURAICH (Bay of the Coracle), on the southern shore, a little to the east of Port Laraichean, is the historic bay where Columba first landed in Iona with his twelve companions. It is flanked with high rocks, and is divided in two by a low rock islet, which forms a kind of natural pier when the weather and tide are favourable. The east side is Port na Curaich proper.

Columba is said to have buried his coracle on the beach, and a long, grassy mound at the head of the bay was commonly believed to conceal the relic. Recent excavations, however, revealed nothing; and it is now suggested that this is one of the " long-barrows " or grave-mounds of the Stone Age.

A number of cairns have been piled up at the western end of the beach. Pennant, who saw a vast tract of them hereabouts, says that they were believed to be the penances of monks. Reeves thinks they are probably sepulchral, and Trenholme suggests that this was the cemetery of the men who lived in Port Laraichean.

The beach below is strewn with coloured pebbles of great variety and beauty, and on a sunny day, when the tide is receding, they sparkle and glow like Eastern gems.

Out in the bay, there is a reef of translucent green serpentine from which tiny fragments are broken off and cast ashore by the waves. These pebbles, which are becoming rarer, are known as Iona stone, or St. Columba's stone, and are reputed to be a charm against drowning.

THE MARBLE QUARRY. Reference has been made to the Iona marble, a fine, ornamental stone of white veined with the green of the mineral serpentine, and suited in our climate for internal but not external use. It is " an ophicalite, resembling the green Connemara marble and the Verde Antico of the ancients " (*The Quarry*, December, 1907). The quarry is at the foot of a ravine, facing the Sound, and not far from the south-western extremity of the island; and its position—shut in as it is by cliff and boulder, and giving on to an inhospitable shore — makes the difficulties of transit almost insurmountable.

PIGEONS' CAVE. To reach the Pigeons' Cave, which is at the foot of the next ravine, slightly farther north, the pedestrian should turn down a grassy ravine, just opposite to the Sound of Erraid, and he will find the entrance hidden among the rocks to the right. As its name signifies, the cave is the haunt of the wild pigeon. It is 40 yards long, and has a sandy bottom. There is a second cave beside it, nearer the sea.

LOCH STAONAIG is the name of a marshy loch that one is likely to encounter while crossing the island to explore the southern shore. It lies about the middle of the southern tract.

MARTYRS' BAY lies not far south of the village. On its southern promontory stands the little Free Kirk (as it was originally) which with its modest dimensions and innocence of art strikes perhaps a more harmonious note than the mediæval Abbey in the island of Columba. Tradition associates this spot with the first recorded slaughter of the monks by the Danes in 806.

It was to this little port that the galleys and barges of old brought the distinguished dead. Opposite the bay is a low, green mound called Ealadh, and here the bodies were laid for a space, while the mourners gathered round " to pour their wailing over the dead ".

THE STREET OF THE DEAD. This is the traditional name of the road that led from Martyrs' Bay to Reilig Odhrain, and marked the route of the funeral trains of old.

IX

Conclusion

This, then, is the Iona of Columba.

" There is the bay where the little, sea-tossed coracle drove ashore. There is the hill —the Hill of Angels—where heavenly visitants shone before him. There is the sound across which the men of Mull heard vespers sung by hooded monks—heard the Lord's song sung in a strange land. There is the narrow strip of water across which holy men came to take counsel, sinners to do penance, kings to be crowned. The little island speaks with a quiet insistence of its past—for was it not at once the fountain and the fortress of the faith, at once the centre of Celtic learning and of Christian charity?"—(Troup).

" The mountaineer and the fisherman and the shepherd of the Isles live their lives in lonely places, and the winds and waves bear to them messages from the unknown beyond. They hear the tide of Eternity forever breaking round the coasts of time, and in spirit they, like St. Brendan, voyage far in fairy seas. . . .

" Part of the inheritance of the Celt is the sense of the longing and striving after the unattainable and incomprehensible on Earth. . . . Forlorn, he has the sense of fighting a losing battle for all his soul holds dear; for the simple life of old, for the beauty of the world threatened with utilitarian desecration, for outlived ideals of love and faith and loyalty, of honour and of chivalry."—(Wilkie).

" As I write, here on the hill-slope of Dùn-I, the sound of the furtive wave is as the sighing in a shell. I am alone between sea and sky, for there is no other on this bouldered height, nothing visible but a single blue shadow that slowly sails the hill-side. The bleating of the lambs and ewes, the lowing of kine, these come up from the Machair that lies between the west slopes and the shoreless sea to the west; these ascend as the very smoke of sound. All around the island there is a continuous breathing; deeper and more prolonged on the west, where the open sea is, but audible everywhere. The seals on Soa are even now putting their breasts against the running tide; for I see a flashing of fins here and there in patches at the north end of the Sound, and already from the ruddy granite shores of the Ross there is a congregation of sea-fowl—gannets and guillemots, skuas and herring-gulls, the long-necked northern diver, the tern, the cormorant. In the sunblaze,

the waters of the Sound dance their blue bodies
and swirl their flashing white hair o' foam; and,
as I look, they seem to me like children of the
wind and the sunshine, leaping and running in
these flowing pastures, with a laughter as sweet
against the ears as the voices of children at play.

" The joy of life vibrates everywhere. . . .
Not a stone's throw from where I lie, half-
hidden beneath an overhanging rock is the Pool
of Healing. To this small, black-brown tarn,
pilgrims of every generation, for hundreds of
years, have come. Solitary, these; not only
because the pilgrim to the Fount of Eternal
Youth must fare hither alone, and at dawn,
so as to touch the healing water the moment
the first sunray quickens it—but solitary, also,
because those who go in quest of this Fount
of Youth are the dreamers and the Children of
Dream, and these are not many, and few come
now to this lonely place. Yet an Isle of Dream
Iona is, indeed. Here the last sun-worshippers
bowed before the rising of God; here Columba
and his hymning priests laboured and brooded
. . . here, for century after century, the Gael
has lived, suffered, joyed, dreamed his impossible, beautiful dream; as here, now, he still
lives, still suffers patiently, still dreams, and
through all and over all, broods upon the
incalculable mysteries. He is an elemental,
among the elemental forces. He knows the

voices of wind and sea; and it is because the Fount of Youth upon Dùn-I of Iona is not the only well-spring of peace, that the Gael can confront his destiny as he does, and can endure. . . . For the genius of the Celtic race stands out now with averted touch, and the light of it is as a glory before the eyes, and the flame of it is blown into the hearts of the stronger people. The Celt fades, but his spirit rises in the heart and the mind of the Anglo-Celtic peoples, with whom are the destinies of generations to come.

"I stop, and look sea-ward from this hill-slope of Dùn-I. Yes, even in this Isle of Joy, as it seems in this dazzle of golden light and splashing wave, there is the like mortal gloom and immortal mystery which moved the minds of the old seers and bards. Yonder, where that thin spray quivers against the thyme-set cliff, is the Spouting Cave, where to this day the Mar-Tarbh, dread creature of the sea, swims at the full of the tide. Beyond, out of sight behind these craggy steeps, is Port na Curaich, where, a thousand years ago, Columba landed in his coracle. Here, eastward, is the landing-place for the dead of old, brought hence out of Christendom for sacred burial in the Isle of the Saints. All the story of the Gael is here. Iona is the microcosm of the Gaelic world."
—(Fiona Macleod).

An ancient prophecy attributed to Columba, and cherished by all lovers of Iona, runs as follows:—

> " An I mo chridhe, I mo ghràidh,
>   An àite guth mhanach bidh geum bà;
>   Ach mu'n tig an savghal gu crìch,
>   Bithidh I mar a bha ".

> " In Iona of my heart, Iona of my love,
>   Instead of monk's voice shall be lowing of cows;
>   But ere the world shall come to an end,
>   Iona shall be as it was."

NOTE ON THE ILLUMINATED MANUSCRIPTS

There is a legend, sometimes scoffed at, that some of the pigments used by the monks of Iona were brought all the way from Mount Athos in Greece. Corroboration, however, has been received by the author from an archæologist attached to the British School at Athens who spent several weeks on Mount Athos and was especially interested in pigments.

Staffa. Fingal's Cave on the right:
Boat Cave in the centre

Lagandoran Sands

APPENDIX I

The Neighbouring Isles and Staffa

The numerous islets lying off Iona are more or less of similar aspect: bird-haunted rocks, grown over with turf and heather, appearing at first sight barren and devoid of interest, but in reality possessing a peculiar charm which only intimate acquaintance can reveal. On a diminutive scale they are full of feature, for nature, whose hand alone has touched them, abhors monotony. Each has its particular view-point of the wide, Hebridean seas and skies. Each, too, has its population, its little life of small, shy creatures that haunt beach and bog and meadow, and, as in the remoter Orkneys, its surface " is ever beat upon by soft, soundless feet and shadowed by swiftly moving wings, and many a little comedy or tragedy is played out upon its stage. We walk upon it in spring or summer through an air fragrant with the perfume of innumerable small, sweet flowers, with the music of birds and bees about us, and ever. under and behind all song, the voice of the great sea, full of undefinable mystery, as of a half-remembered dream " (Duncan Robertson).

EILEAN CHALMAIN, off the southern extremity of the Ross of Mull, is one of the most charming of these islets, especially in early spring, when it is festive with wild flowers. In autumn it yields a rich harvest of brambles.

EILEAN NAM MUC (Isle of Pigs (? Sea-pigs or Whales)) takes its name from a species of seal that used to haunt its shores. In the month of August the island is white with the heather that is said to bring luck to all finders; but unfortunately the vandals amongst the yearly visitors are reducing the carpet to patchwork.

EILEAN NA H'AON CHAORACH (Island of One Sheep) lies south of Port na-Curaich. The name gives the measure of the islet's pasturage.

EILEAN NAM BĂN (The Women's Island) lies close to the Mull shore, just opposite to the Iona ruins. To this place, tradition says, Columba banished all women and cows from Iona for a reason preserved in the old distich:

> Far am bi bo bidh bean,
> S' far am bi bean bidh mallachadh.

> Where there is a cow,
> There will be a woman;
> And where there is a woman,
> There will be mischief.

Probably the island was set apart for the wives of labourers employed by the monks.

SOA, which lies well off the southern shore of Iona, was in early times the monastery seal-farm, which helped to supply the table on fast days. Adamnan relates how a thief named Erc hid on the shore of Mull " that by night he might sail over to the little island where the sea-calves, ours by right, are bred and breed ". Seals still make their home on the lonely islet, and their movements may be studied here at close quarters.

ERRAID is a larger island—practically an isthmus at low tide—close to the Ross. The relief men for the Dhu Hearteach lighthouse are stationed here, and signal twice daily to the men on duty, fifteen miles south-west. Robert Louis Stevenson once spent some time on the island, and David Balfour, the hero of his *Kidnapped*, is wrecked on its shore at the beginning of his adventurous journey across country.

From the high ground of Erraid there is a fine view of the southern isles.

MULL is one of the largest islands in the Hebrides, and is so indented with bays and sea lochs that though its greatest length is only thirty-five miles, its circumference is actually three hundred.

The Ross, or south-western extremity, off which Iona lies, is unimposing in line, but has great beauty of colour. The picturesque hamlets of Fionphort and Kintra are within easy boating distance, but finer far is the sail through dark Loch Scridain, on the inner side of the rocky headland Bourg, to Pennyghael, whence the road to Salen traverses some of the wildest and grandest country in Scotland. The squalls that descend frequently from the hills to the loch give a spice of adventure to the trip (and, incidentally, call for oilskins). Near the head of the loch, the ascent of Ben More (3097 feet) may be made. This country is the scene of William Black's *Macleod of Dare*.

The outer side of the Bourg is also well worth exploring. Myriads of cormorants nest in the shelving rocks, and wild goats wander on the grassy slopes below. A fine cave, known as Mackinnon's, lies a little south of the Isle of Inch Kenneth, where Dr. Johnson and Boswell once spent a night.

Other islands within reach by open boat—though the remoter ones should be attempted only in the most favourable weather—are Ulva, a name familiar to readers of Campbell's *Lord Ullin's Daughter*; Gometra, close by Ulva; the lonely Treshnish Islands, including the quaintly-shaped Dutchman's Cap; Tiree, closely associated with the ecclesiastical history of Iona; and Staffa, which is described separately.

STAFFA (Stafr-ey, the Isle of Staves or Columns) is a rocky islet about one and a half miles in circumference, lying eight miles north of Iona.

In the remote past, the north-west coast of Scotland was the scene of violent volcanic action, which has left traces along the west coast, in a line extending from Skye to the Giant's Causeway in Ireland. In consequence of the subterranean disturbances, large volumes of liquid basalt were thrown forth, which, when it began to cool, formed in Staffa, as elsewhere, tiers of columns, curiously symmetrical in shape and size. The action of the waves and the weather throughout the centuries that followed created the amazing caverns of Staffa—

> " Where as to shame the temples decked
>   By skill of earthly architect,
> Nature herself, it seemed, would raise
>   A Minster to her Maker's praise."
>   —*Sir Walter Scott.*

Fingal's Cave, the " Minster " of the above lines, is the largest of the caves, and, as a rule, the only one visited. Its old Gaelic name is " Uamh Bhinn ", the Melodious Cavern. The grandeur and solemnity of this mighty cavern cannot be fully realized amongst the motley crowd in which the majority of visitors make their approach. " How could we feel it?" asked Wordsworth; " each the other's blight."

> " One votary at will might stand
>   Gazing, and take into his mind and heart,
>   With undistracted reverence, the effect
> Of those proportions where the Almighty Hand
> That made the worlds, the Sovereign Architect,
> Had deigned to work as if with human Art."

The height of the great arch, at mean tide, is sixty-six feet; the depth of the sea below is about the same; and the cliff above rises a further thirty feet. The length is two hundred and twenty-seven feet—half as much again as that of Iona Abbey Church. The sides, at the entrance, are vertical and nearly parallel, and are composed of black, basaltic pillars, of which the majority are pentagonal or hexagonal in form, and divided transversely by joints, like the columns of ancient Greek temples, at almost equal distances of two feet. The lights that tremble and flicker over the pillars reveal in the dark basalt warm tints of red and brown and russet; here and there the rock is crusted with gold and green lichen, and the depths of the clear green sea below abound with polyps and the beautiful blue medusæ. A constant boom, as of distant thunder, fills the air as the Atlantic swell bursts into the cave, and the voices of the sea-birds ring high and clear above the tumult. Here, one feels, in the ocean solitudes, the elemental forces have hewn a temple of wild and noble splendour, wherein to worship the Power that rules them; and the awed observer perforce bows with them.

" I have seen the temple not made with hands," wrote Sir Robert Peel, after a visit to Staffa, " and have felt the majestic swell of the ocean—the pulsation of the great Atlantic—beating in its inmost sanctuary, and swelling a note of praise nobler far than any that ever pealed from human organ."

From the landing-place to the top of the island, a stair has been formed, and glimpses of the cliffs and caves on the other side of the island may be obtained. The Boat Cave, accessible only by sea, is one hundred and fifty feet long; the Cormorants', or Mackinnon's, is two hundred and twenty feet in length, and fifty in height at the entrance; the Clam Shell is smaller, but is interesting because of its shape, the columns being bent like ship's timbers.

Not far from Fingal's Cave is the Giant's Colonnade—

an islet formed of a group of columns about 30 feet high,
and well worthy of inspection.

APPENDIX II
Chronological Table

Approximate dates are marked " c " (*circa*). Events not directly
connected with the island are in square brackets.

368	[Last Roman Invasion of Scotland.]
432	[Death of St. Ninian.]
441	[Death of St. Patrick.]
500–600	[Conquest of Dalriada by the Scots.]
	[Conquest of the Lothians by the Angles of Northumbria.]
514	[Birth of St. Kentigern.]
521	Birth of St. Columba.
563	12th May. Columba lands in Iona.
565	Conversion of Northern Picts.
571	[Birth of Mahomet.]
574	Columba consecrates Aidan King of Dalriadic Scots, in Iona. First Coronation in Britain.
575	Convention of Drumceatt.
c 580	Cormac's missionary journey to Orkney.
	Monastery of Deer (Aberdeenshire) founded by St. Columba and St. Drostan.
590	[Gregory the Great, Pope.]
597	Sunday, 9th June. Death of Columba.
	[Augustine lands in Kent.]

597–600   Baithne, Columba's cousin, 2nd Abbot.

600–605   Laisren, 3rd Abbot.

605–623   Fergna, 4th Abbot.

617   Slaughter of St. Donnan and fifty-two monks
           on the Isle of Eigg, at instigation of a
           Pictish Queen.

623–652   Seghine, 5th Abbot.

627   [Paulinus converts Edwin, King of Northum-
           bria.]

           [Pagan reaction in Northumbria.]

           Oswald, Edwin's heir, educated in Iona.

653   Iona mission to Northumbria. Aidan founds
           monastery of Lindisfarne.

652–657   Suibhne, 6th Abbot.

657–669   Cummian the Fair, 7th Abbot.   Wrote *On
           the Virtues of St. Columba*.

664   Synod of Whitby.   Northumbria adopts
           Roman Christianity.

669–679   Failbhe, 8th Abbot.

679–704   Adamnan, 9th Abbot. Paschal controversy
           becomes acute.

           Life of St. Columba written by Adamnan.

           Brude, King of Picts, buried in Iona.

685   Egfrid, King of Northumbria, buried in
           Iona.

687   Monastery repaired at expense of King of
           Dalriada.

704–710   Conamhail, 10th Abbot.

710–717   Dunchadh, 11th Abbot.

716   Iona adopts Roman Easter.

717–724   Faelcu, 12th Abbot.

717   Expulsion of Columban Monks by Naiton,
                    King of Picts.

724–726   Cillene Fada (Cillen the Tall), 13th Abbot.

726–752   Cillene Droicteach (Cillen the Bridgemaker),
                    14th Abbot.

                (?) Causeway built across the Lochan Mor.

749   " A great wind. The drowning of the Family
                    of Ia." (*Irish Chronicle.*)

752–767   Slebhine, 15th Abbot.

767–772   Suibhne, 16th Abbot.

772–801   Breasal, 17th Abbot.

                Two Irish ex-kings, Iona monks, buried in
                    Iona.

787   [Order of Culdees founded by St. Mael-
                    ruain.]

797   Iona sacked by Danes.

800   Norse settlements in Scotland begin. Culdees
                    spread to Scotland from Ireland.

801–802   Connachtach, 18th Abbot. " Scriba selectis-
                    simus."

                Monastery burned by Danes.

802–815   Cellach, 19th Abbot.

                Columba's remains enshrined.

806   Massacre of sixty-eight monks by Danes,
                    traditionally at Martyrs' Bay.

814   Primacy transferred to Kells in Ireland.

815–832   Dermid, 20th Abbot.

c 818   Primacy transferred from Kells to Dunkeld.

825   19th January, Danish massacre on Iona, com-
                    memorated as Passion of St. Blathmac and
                    the Martyrs of Iona.

844	[Kenneth Macalpine, first king of a united Scotland.]
832–854	Innrechtach, 21st Abbot.
c 844	Coronation stone brought from Argyll to Scone.
854	Succession of resident Abbots broken.
860	Kenneth Macalpine buried in Iona.
863	Donald I buried in Iona.
c 870	Western Isles subdued by Norwegians.
877	Constantine I buried in Iona.
878	King Aedh buried in Iona.
c 889	King Ging buried in Iona.
900	Donald II buried in Iona.
908	Primacy transferred to St. Andrews.
954	Malcolm I buried in Iona.
963	King Indulf buried in Iona.
967	King Duff buried in Iona.
976	Shrine of St. Columba robbed.
980	Anlaf, King of Danes, comes to end days in Iona.
986	Massacre of Abbots and fifteen monks by Danes, traditionally on the White Sands.
997	Constantine III buried in Iona.
1018	[Malcolm II defeats the Northumbrians at Carham, and annexes the Lothians.]
1034	Malcolm II buried in Iona.
	Eleventh Century. Iona under Norwegian Diocese of Man and the Isles.
1040	King Duncan buried in Iona.
1057	Macbeth buried in Iona.
	Lulach the Fatuous buried in Iona.

1070	[Marriage of Malcolm Canmore to Saxon Princess, Margaret.]
1072	Malcolm and Margaret visit Iona. [Establishment of Roman Christianity in Scotland.]
1093	[Celtic reaction.]
1096	[First Crusade.]
1097	King Magnus of Norway visits Iona.
1124	[David I succeeds to throne.] Latinizing of Scottish Church resumed.
1154	Diocese of Man and the Isles placed under Trondjem (Norway).
1164	After sixty-five years silence, mention of deputation from Iona to Ireland. Presence of Culdees on Iona first recorded.
c 1175	William the Lion grants Iona's Lowland Churches and titles in Galloway to Holyrood.
1188	[Pope Clement III declares Scottish Church independent of English Church.] Godred, Norse King of Man, buried in Iona.
c 1200	Family of Hy ousted from Iona after tenure of 640 years. Reginald, Lord of the Isles, establishes Monastery of Black Monks and a community of Black Nuns (Benedictines) on Iona.
1203	Pope Clement III takes Iona community under his protection.
1210	Iona plundered by Norwegian pirates.
1263	[Defeat of Haco of Norway at Battle of Largs.]

1266 Norway cedes Hebrides to Scotland. Iona under Dunkeld.

1314 [Battle of Bannockburn.]

c 1500 Iona Abbey becomes Cathedral.

1542 [Accession of Mary, Queen of Scots.]

1549 Donald Monro, Dean of the Isles, visits Iona.

1560 [Reformation. Adoption of Protestantism by Scottish Church.]

1561 Monks expelled from Iona.

1574 Nuns expelled from Iona.
Iona passes to Macleans of Duart.

1603 [Union of Crowns of England and Scotland.]

1609 Statutes of Icolmkill drawn up in Iona.

1610 [First temporary Episcopacy.]

1635 Charles I orders grant of £400 for the restoration of Iona Cathedral.

1638 [Signature of National Covenant. Abolition of Episcopacy.]

1661 [Second temporary Episcopacy.]

1688 Sacheverell visits Iona.

1690 [Re-establishment of Presbytery.]

1693 Iona passes from Maclean of Duart to Duke of Argyll.

1745 Iona men fight with Maclean for Prince Charles.

1772 Pennant visits Iona.

1773 Dr. Johnson and Boswell visit Iona.

1843 [Disruption of Church of Scotland.]

1899   Iona Abbey given in trust to the Church of Scotland by George, eighth Duke of Argyll. (By the terms of the Trust Deed, it is provided that any recognized Christian denomination can apply for its use for the celebration of its full office of worship. " It thus becomes the only Church building, known to us, in Christendom where no Christians are guests but all can claim to be at home." *Behold Iona.*)

1900   [Union of Free and United Presbyterian Churches of Scotland.]

1905   Restoration of Abbey Church completed.

1929   [Union of Church of Scotland and United Free Church.]

1938   The Iona Community, a Brotherhood of Ministers and Men, founded by the Rev. George Macleod, D.D.

1940   Chapter House and Library above restored by the Iona Community.

1947   Eamonn de Valera visits Iona.

1950   The Archbishop of Dublin visits Iona.

        The Archbishop of York visits Iona.

1956   Queen Elizabeth, the Duke of Edinburgh and Princess Margaret visit Iona.

1956–7   Excavations on the site of the Columban foundation carried out.

1957   Excavators discover what is believed to be the long-lost cell of St. Columba.

APPENDIX III

Bibliography

(*Arranged Chronologically*)

Approximate dates are marked " c " (*circa*). Titles of books not directly concerned with Iona are in square brackets.

c 700   Adamnan (*ob.* 704)—Vita Sanctae Columbae. Trans. W. Huyshe. (Routledge's Shiling Library.)

Bede (*ob.* 735)—Opera Historica. Plummer, 1896.

900–1000 Irish Life of St. Columba. Trans. from the Leabhar Breac, in Skene's Celtic Scotland.

1187   [Chronicles of the Scots and Picts. Skene's edition, 1867.]

1251   [Chronicle of the Picts and Scots. Skene's edition, 1867.]

1400–1500 [Annals of Ulster. Ed. by Henessy and Macarthy, 1901.]

1549   Monro's Account in Macfarlane MSS. (Advocate's Library). Early MS. in Switzerland.

1600–1700 [Annals of Ireland by the Four Masters. Compiled from older sources in the seventeenth century. Ed. by O'Donovan, 1856.]

1702   Sacheverell—An Account of the Isle of Man, with a Voyage to Icolmkill in the year 1688.

1703   Martin's Description of Western Isles.

1774   Pennant—Voyage to the Hebrides.

1785   Boswell—Journal of a Tour to the Hebrides
              with Samuel Johnson—Carruther's Edi-
              tion, 1852.

1833-41   Maclean's Historical Account of Iona.

1834   Transactions of Iona Club.

1850   Graham—Antiquities of Iona.

1872   Ewing (Bishop)—Iona.

1875   Skene—Notes on the Earlier Establishments at
              Iona. In Proceedings of Society of Anti-
              quaries of Scotland, 1875.

1876   Skene—Notes on the History of the Ruins at
              Iona. P.S.A.S., 1876.

1878   Argyll (Duke of)—Iona.

1881   Drummond—Sculptured Monuments in Iona
              and the Western Highlands.

1881   [Warren—Liturgy and Ritual of the Celtic
              Church.]

1890   [Skene—Celtic Scotland.]

1893   Wilson—Guide to Staffa and Iona.

1894   [Dowden—Celtic Church in Scotland.]

            [Stephen—History of the Scottish Church.]

1896   [McGibbon and Ross—Ecclesiastical Archi-
              tecture of Scotland.]

1898   Macmillan and Brydall—Iona: Its History and
              Antiquities.

1900   Macleod (Fiona)—Iona (with other essays).

1903   [Geikie (A.)—Text-book of Geology.]

1904   [Allen—Celtic Art in Pagan and Christian
              Times.]

1909   Trenholme (E. C.)—The Story of Iona.

1913   Troup, G. E.—Monograph, Saint Columba, The Lord's Song in a Strange Land. Edinburgh, 1913.

1920   Lucy Menzies—St. Columba of Iona.

1928   A. and E. Ritchie—Map of Iona, republished (1934) as " Iona Past and Present ".

N.B.—For further insight into the Celtic spirit, for which Iona stands, the " Carmina Gadelica ", collected and annotated by Alexander Carmichael, and Campbell's " Tales of the West Highlands " are of the greatest value, whilst amateurs of art should study in one of the bigger libraries, facsimiles of Celtic manuscripts, such as the Books of Durrow and Kells, and amateurs of music the volumes of ancient songs, " Songs of the Hebrides " (Boosey & Co.), collected up and down the Isles by Marjorie Kennedy-Fraser (whose ashes lie in Iona) and Kenneth Macleod.

APPENDIX IV

Some Useful Addresses

St. Columba Hotel. Proprietor: Mr. Walter Tindal.

Argyll Hotel. Proprietrix: Mrs. Campbell.

Traighmore (Guest House): Miss Cameron.

Culbhuirg (Guest House): Mrs. MacInnes.

Bishop's Walk (Guest House): Mrs. Macfarlane.

Sithean (Guest House): Mrs. MacCormick.

Highland Home Industries (Iona Celtic Jewellery): Mrs. MacCormick.

Handloom Weaving: William Macdonald, Victoria Cottage.

Post Office: Miss Macphail.

Postal Address: Iona, by Oban.

Scottish Tourist Board: 2 Rutland Place, Edinburgh.

INDEX

OF ANTIQUITIES AND TOPOGRAPHY